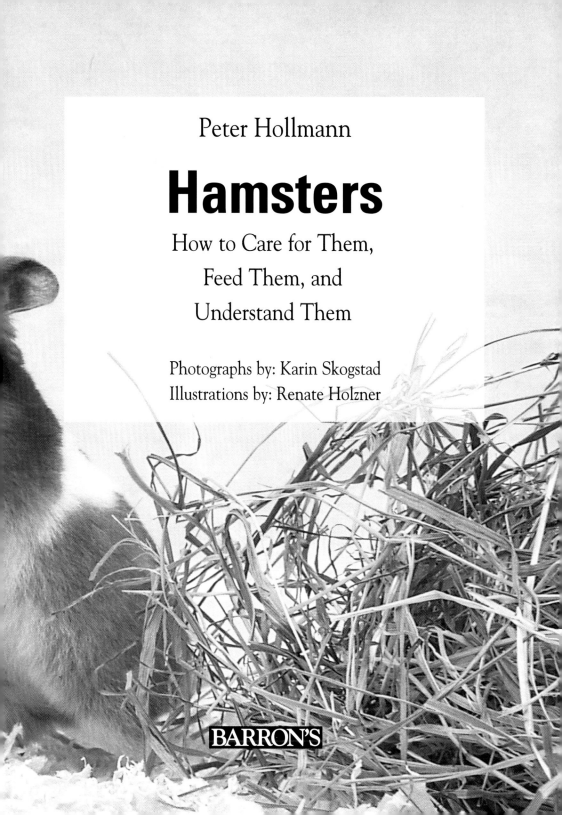

Peter Hollmann

Hamsters

How to Care for Them,
Feed Them, and
Understand Them

Photographs by: Karin Skogstad
Illustrations by: Renate Holzner

BARRON'S

C O N T E N T S

What You Should Know Before Getting a Hamster

The cute hamster has long been a favorite house pet even though it sleeps through the entire day and doesn't become active until evening.

Where Hamsters Feel Comfortable

People who want a hamster for a house pet usually think first of the Syrian golden hamster. But for some years pet shops also have been offering Chinese dwarf and striped hamsters, Djungarian hamsters, and Roborowski dwarf hamsters.

The Hamster's Home

Simplicity, robustness, and adaptability are some of the qualities all hamsters have. It's easy to understand where these qualities originated if you take a look at the history of this little rodent.

The natural environment to which wild hamsters are well adapted is the desert. Because it rarely rains there, vegetation is correspondingly sparse, but no matter—hamsters are hardy creatures that can get by on very little. Their brownish coats that match the color of the desert floor are another indication of their origin in the sand and steppes of the Old World, from Central Europe to Asia. The area of distribution of the Syrian

Fresh twigs from fruit and deciduous trees are very desirable as gnawing material.

Hamsters like to use clay pots like this one as hiding places.

golden hamster (*Mesocricetus auratus*) encompasses the arid regions of Bulgaria, Romania, Asia Minor, the Caucasus, Syria, Israel, and Iran.

The Chinese dwarf or striped hamster (*Cricetulus griseus*) inhabits the Chinese and Mongolian semidesert in Central Asia.

The steppes of Kazakhstan, Manchuria, and Mongolia are home to the Djungarian dwarf hamster (*Phodopus sungorus*).

The Roborowski dwarf hamster (*Phodopus roborovskii*) lives in the regions of Mongolia that border China and in parts of Siberia.

Hamsters as House Pets

Like most small rodents that are kept as house pets today, hamsters were first domesticated to serve as laboratory animals. Their trouble-free breeding and their comical, animated nature, coupled with a reasonable purchase price and a lack of legal restrictions, have paved the way for their worldwide distribution as house pets.

This is especially true for the Syrian golden hamster.

The history of the golden hamster's domestication began when it was first described in 1839 by the naturalist George R. Waterhouse. In April of 1930, near Aleppo in northern Syria, zoologist Israel Aharoni captured a female golden hamster and her twelve young by digging them out of a burrow eight feet deep. He brought his find to the Zoological Institute at the University of Jerusalem. Although only three of the original animals survived the move and life in captivity, within a year Dr. Aharoni had succeeded in raising more than three hundred young. All generations of golden hamsters under human care have come from these animals. In 1938 the first golden hamsters were brought to America as research animals. They didn't arrive in Europe until after World War II.

The Chinese dwarf or banded hamster likewise was first used for laboratory experiments before it became a house pet. The Djungarian dwarf hamster and the Roborowski dwarf hamster began as souvenirs of research trips. Prolific breeders, their progeny eventually showed up in specialty pet shops.

T I P

To better understand hamsters, you should know some biological facts about them (see page 11). Their place in the animal classification system provides information about their nearest relatives (see The Zoological Classification System, page 34).

Hamsters love to work out on their exercise wheel.

Biological Profile of the Hamster

Behavior	Rodent, herbivore, active at dusk and during the night, predominantly a loner			
Size (Length: Head & body)	Syrian golden hamster: 6 to 7 inches	Chinese dwarf or striped hamster: 3 to 5 inches	Djungarian dwarf hamster: 2.75 to 4 inches	Roborowski dwarf hamster: 2.75 to 3.5 inches
Body Weight	Syrian golden hamster: 3 to 6 ounces	Chinese dwarf or striped hamster: 1.2 to 1.6 ounces	Djungarian dwarf hamster: 1.2 to 1.75 ounces	Roborowski dwarf hamster: 1 to 1.4 ounces
Life Expectancy	2 to 3 years			
Sexual Maturity	Syrian golden hamster: 35 to 45 days	Chinese dwarf or striped hamster: 28 to 30 days	Djungarian dwarf hamster: 18 to 23 days	Roborowski dwarf hamster: 14 to 24 days
Breeding Age	3 to 4 months			
Length of Cycle	4 days			
Gestation Period	Syrian golden hamster: 15 to 16 days	Chinese dwarf or striped hamster: 20 to 22 days	Djungarian dwarf hamster: 20 to 22 days	Roborowski dwarf hamster: 19 to 22 days
Birth	Trouble-free delivery, babies from .3 to .6 ounce, bald and blind			
Size of Litter	Syrian golden hamster: 4 to 6	Chinese dwarf or striped hamster: 4 to 7	Djungarian dwarf hamster: 2 to 10	Roborowski dwarf hamster: 1 to 7
Number of Litters per Year	Syrian golden hamster: 4 to 6	Chinese dwarf or striped hamster: 4 to 7	Djungarian dwarf hamster: 3 to 4	Roborowski dwarf hamster: 3 to 4
Age at Weaning	21 days			

Is There Room in Your Life for a Hamster?

Not everyone likes dogs and cats, but there is scarcely a child or adult who is not attracted by the charm of cute little puppies and kittens. One reason people love hamsters is that even in adulthood they retain their cute, baby-like look. The hamster's large head, big, round eyes, and chubby cheeks remind adults of a young child or perhaps a teddy bear. The soft, attractively colored fur of hamsters invites petting and cuddling.

Not a Living Toy

If you want a house pet, you should never get one on the spur of the moment, under the spell of the display window, or because the kids are whining and insist that they have to have an animal right away. Because hamsters are so cute and inexpensive, it's a great temptation to pick one up as you pass the pet shop on the way home from the supermarket. Aside from the fact that after a day or two people often regret a hasty purchase, it is irresponsible to bring a living creature home without knowing anything about it. You can't return or recycle an animal as if it were a toy or a piece of furniture. Our pet animals are always there for us and they deserve the same from us. In return, hamsters give us the opportunity to watch their carefree antics, learn about their behavior, and bond with them—especially because they are so lovable.

Hamsters Are Still Wild Animals

We should never forget that in contrast to dogs and cats, hamsters aren't totally domesticated and still exhibit wild animal-like behavior. They have changed their habits only slightly. Even though they have been bred and kept by humans in houses for generations, it's not possible to have the same type of person-animal bonding you can have with most house pets.

This means that they have a limited capacity for interacting with people and taking part in human life. Anybody for whom that's important should get a more responsive pet. And people who simply want something to cuddle and fondle should get a stuffed animal toy.

Hamsters in a cloud of cotton. Lint is ideal for lining the nest (see page 55).

Fun to Watch

Above all, hamsters are house pets for people who enjoy watching their antics. This is especially true for the tiny weasel-quick dwarf hamsters (see Hamster Breeds, page 34). There are other considerations as well.

Unlike dogs and cats that occupy the same habitat as their human owners, hamsters have their own living space. You will need to provide your hamster with a cage large enough for it to get the exercise it needs and with room enough for a spacious house and an artificial burrow in which it can tuck itself

away for a safe, quiet sleep (see page 44).

As an animal that's active at dusk and in the evening, the hamster sleeps during the day and is unresponsive during that time. Since it has to search far and wide for food in the wild, it is accustomed to running around a lot. That's why you have to provide plenty of opportunities for exercise. A hamster lives only two or three years. During this short lifespan, a pair of hamsters can produce more than 20 litters. Unless you are sure you will be able to find homes for all these offspring, it would be advisable to keep just one hamster at a time.

Making Up Your Mind

Before buying a hamster, you should ask yourself the following questions:

1 Can I afford to buy a fairly large cage (see page 44) whose purchase price is out of proportion to the cost of a hamster?

2 Do I have an appropriate place in my home where the hamster can sleep peacefully during the day but make plenty of noise at night without disturbing the rest of the

Should you wake up your hamster?

Hamsters sleep the whole day long. Only in the evening do they emerge from their house. Then they are hungry; they eagerly carry food in their cheek pouches into their house and merrily romp about the cage.

When Timmy got a golden hamster, he knew nothing about the animal. As soon as he got home from school, he would run over to the hamster cage. Of course the hamster would be asleep in its little house. But Timmy really wanted to play with his hamster. He would stick his fingers into the house to get the little rodent out of its hiding place. The hamster would come out grumpy. It even bit Timmy's fingers hard several times. Timmy was disappointed with his pet. One day Timmy noticed that the once shiny coat of his golden hamster had lost its luster. The animal looked at Timmy with dull eyes. In the evening when the little golden hamster came out of its house, it was noticeably shaky as it ran around. Sometimes its entire body shuddered. One morning it lay dead in the cage. That is what will happen to a hamster that is frequently disturbed in its daytime sleep. For that reason you should never wake a sleeping hamster.

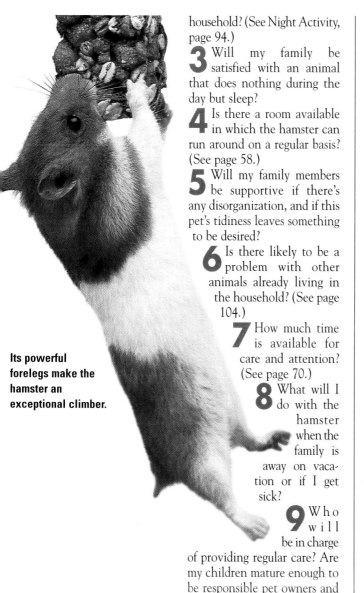

Its powerful
forelegs make the
hamster an
exceptional climber.

household? (See Night Activity, page 94.)

3 Will my family be satisfied with an animal that does nothing during the day but sleep?

4 Is there a room available in which the hamster can run around on a regular basis? (See page 58.)

5 Will my family members be supportive if there's any disorganization, and if this pet's tidiness leaves something to be desired?

6 Is there likely to be a problem with other animals already living in the household? (See page 104.)

7 How much time is available for care and attention? (See page 70.)

8 What will I do with the hamster when the family is away on vacation or if I get sick?

9 Who will be in charge of providing regular care? Are my children mature enough to be responsible pet owners and

pitch in. to help care for our hamster? (See page 21.)

10 Is there a member of the family allergic to animal hair? (See page 127.)

The Right Way to Keep a Hamster

The foregoing questions can also be connected to the humane treatment of domesticated animals. Anyone who keeps an animal must see to it that

■ the animal is provided with appropriate types and quantities of food

■ the animal's opportunities for appropriate exercise are adequate to prevent pain, avoidable suffering, or harm.

Appropriate care involves observing the rules of veterinary science or other scientific knowledge so that no impairment of bodily functions occurs which can be traced to stress, inadequate food, or an unhealthy environment.

Your hamster depends upon you for the kind of care that enables it to follow its instincts and behave naturally in a safe environment.

There's no better definition of a hamster's needs. Unless you are sure that you will need nothing from your hamster except to enjoy watching it

thrive in the best environment you can provide for it, then you should think about getting a different kind of pet.

Who Should Have a Hamster?

Hamsters are suited primarily to working people who take pleasure in returning home in the evening to a comical, enterprising roommate. A hamster also doesn't take it badly if its playtime is occasionally canceled because of time restrictions. Finally, hamsters are appropriate pets for people who have only a small apartment, for in contrast to many other pets, they require very little space.

Children and Hamsters

If you would like to give your children a hamster, they should be at least ten years old. By that time, children are in a position to understand the animal's needs.

Hamsters are asleep at the precise time when children want to play with them.

Extensive grooming is a gauge of well-being in hamsters.

The head is subjected to an intensive grooming procedure.

Conversely, children have to go to bed when hamsters are most active.

Furthermore, children should be told at the time of purchase that their little friend will grow old in a much shorter time than humans or even cats and dogs do. On one hand, this is a major disadvantage because the two or three years of a hamster's life go by very quickly, and the separation can be very painful. On the other hand, as children grow older they often lose interest in their independent, some- what unsociable companion.

In that case, the hamster's short life span will enable you and your children to move on to a larger, more sociable pet. Perhaps these observations strike you as a little unfeeling, but they reflect my practical experience as a veterinarian. The hamster's inevitable demise will teach your children lessons about life's seasons. They will learn that all things come to an end. They will miss their little pet. Then, as time passes, they will start thinking about another pet.

Some Considerations Before Getting a Hamster

In the previous chapter we discussed whether or not a hamster is an appropriate pet for you and your family. Now let's discuss what you should think about before buying a hamster, so that no unpleasant surprises spoil the enjoyment you get from the new housemate.

One Hamster or Two?

In nature, hamsters live as loners. Therefore, as house pets they are suited to being kept alone. In their natural habitat, hamsters require quite a large territory for gathering food because of the scarce vegetation on the steppes or in the desert, and they defend their territory against intruders. The need for their own territory is part of their self-preservation instinct. There is often no room even for a mate.

Only during the mating season do males and females get together. This lasts briefly, though, and they go their own way after a day or two.

In small cages that offer no chance to hide or flee, there can be some violent fights. Although siblings may at first get along well because they carry the same nest scent, they are inclined to fight with one another as they grow older. Usually one of the hamsters becomes dominant and drives the other away from the house or chases it from the food supply. The subordinate

Children must be encouraged to be very gentle in handling hamsters.

Since the hamster's house serves the dual purpose of sleeping quarters and storehouse, it should not be too small. This one is a little snug for this golden hamster.

animal experiences continual stress and greater susceptibility to illness, as well as a shorter life expectancy (see Health Precautions and Illnesses, page 72).

Suggestion: If one of the hamsters sleeps cowering in a corner and makes hissing and squeaking noises at night, the two squabblers must be separated to different cages. Weight loss and ruffled fur are signs that you must act quickly; otherwise the weaker animal will die (see Illnesses, page 73).

Keeping a male and female hamster together is advisable only for breeding purposes. After mating, both hamsters must be separated again. Even two males or two females don't tolerate each other for very long.

Suggestion: The behavior outlined above pertains primarily to golden hamsters. Dwarf hamsters usually tolerate one another better (see page 34).

Keeping busy with food prevents boredom in the cage.

Male or Female?

Usually gender doesn't matter much when you have a single hamster.

Males are slightly more mellow than females and become hand tamed more quickly. That's probably because females are somewhat more distant as a result of their nesting behavior. (See page 90.) But males tend to have problems with obesity, and often emit a strong odor.

All other traits are not attributable to one sex or the other, but are simply the expression of individual differences among animals.

Determining Sex

Although the sexual organs of male and female hamsters are standard, it is common for people to mistake one sex for the other. Then you end up with babies in the nest!

To determine the sex, grasp the hamster with three fingers around the neck and support its bottom with the other hand. Then examine the hamster's underside (see photos on pages 27 and 56).

In males, the distance between the anal opening and the sex organ is greater than in females. Also, males have a pointed bottom. From the fifth week of life on, males exhibit bulging testicles on both sides of the anus.

Suggestion: If you have a definite preference for one sex or the other, it might be a good idea to peek over the shoulder of the pet store clerk to be sure there's no mistake in getting the right sex.

Hamsters: Playmates for Children?

Unlike dogs, hamsters are not ideal playmates for children. It is important to teach children that hamsters are not interested in fetching a stick or chasing a ball. They have no innate desire to be cuddled and should not be handled constantly. Young people should learn to enjoy hamsters by watching their antics, caring for them, and learning about their behavior.

Parents must also explain to their children that an animal is not a toy. You can load a stuffed animal into a little wagon, dress it up, shove it into a box, drag it around any way you want, or toss it aside. But you can't do any of those things with a living animal!

No matter how well-intentioned children are when they

convince their parents to buy the pet, they are usually not dependable when it comes to the routine of caring for a pet. When they buy a hamster, parents must understand clearly that after a while they may have to take over regular care of the new housemate, especially when school creates demands on the children.

With improper handling, a hamster can be badly injured or become agitated, anxious, and aggressive. The life expectancy of an animal under continual stress is short. Catching, picking up, and carrying (see page 108) a hamster without injuring it is difficult for children. Hamsters, especially the smaller ones like the Chinese striped hamster, the Djungarian dwarf hamster, or the Roborowski dwarf hamster (see Hamster Breeds, page 34) are so lightning-quick that they can easily slip through a small child's fingers and be badly hurt in a fall from even a modest height.

Pet Sitting While You're Away?

Even before buying a hamster, you should think about accommodations for it while you are away from the house on vacation or for other reasons.

<u>At home:</u> It is ideal for the hamster to stay in its accustomed surroundings, so try to find a reliable pet sitter who can devote an hour to taking care of your pet every evening. Always leave a short written care guide so that the substitute caregiver will not have to guess about what is required. Also jot down your vacation

Climbing apparatus should never reach any appreciable height, and should always be located over a safe surface in order to avoid injuries from falls.

Can hamsters be housebroken?

Unfortunately not. Hamsters are by nature very clean animals. Several times a day they clean their coat thoroughly. They work the fur with their tongue, teeth, and front paws. In the cage they use a particular corner as a toilet. But when your hamster is running around free in the room, it may leave small dry pellets or a little puddle on the rug.

Under no circumstances should you scold or punish the hamster. That would only make it fearful and shy. Your best bet is to sweep up the pellets or use the vacuum cleaner. Urine is best cleaned up with hot water or a commercial product formulated to remove urine stains and odor.

address and how to contact the veterinarian. Professional pet sitters provide forms for you to fill out with this information.

You should write down where the cage should be; you don't want someone to leave it where it will be in direct sunlight, or near direct heat or air-conditioning.

Instruct your hamster sitter to check your pet's drinking bottle every day to see if it has become clogged, and to be sure to fill it.

Also, tell your sitter not to let the hamster out of the cage— even if he or she is experienced with small pets. Imagine returning from your trip to find that the tiny animal has escaped into the walls!

If other pets, such as dogs or cats, will be in the house while you are gone, it's best to take the hamster with you or leave it with a friend.

Accommodations outside the house: Friends or relatives can take the hamster and care for it. It won't harm a hamster to go for up to two weeks without outside exercise, as long as it is in a properly constructed cage (see The Right Type of Cage, page 44).

Suggestion: There are services that provide care for pets during an owner's absence. You can usually find addresses in the classified section of local newspapers. Better yet, ask a pet-owning friend for a recommendation.

Taking the hamster along on vacation: It is possible to take the hamster along in your car, RV, or camper. But you should consider that a long drive and different environmental conditions may provoke unaccustomed stress in the animal.

23

Legal Issues for Hamster Owners

Purchase Agreement

A reputable breeder or dealer will always take back an ill animal that is returned within a reasonable time—usually 48 hours. A refund or healthy animal is given in exchange. Although this is done as a matter of courtesy and good customer relations, the purchaser should nevertheless be able to prove that the animal was ill at the time of purchase. Although an oral contract is binding, a written purchase agreement is always a good idea.

If, on the other hand, you are planning to give away or sell a hamster, provide a written agreement to the new owner that you will take the pet back if, for any reason, the new owner cannot care for it. This will encourage the new owner to return the hamster, if necessary, to someone who will care for it properly. You should consider yourself responsible for any animal you have acquired through purchase or breeding.

Apartments

If a lease does not include any restrictions pertaining to pet ownership, you may assume that the usual house pets are acceptable. This would be especially true for small animals such as hamsters, which are not like to cause damage or to disturb the peace of neighbors. If, however, you intend to keep a large number of hamsters, it would be a good idea to check your local zoning regulations and ordinances before acquiring your animals.

It's also important to clean your hamster's cage on a daily basis, provide fresh bedding, and remove any vegetables your pet has hoarded in its hiding places. If you fail to do this, the unpleasant odor of rotting organic matter will become a nuisance as it wafts into neighbors' windows and attracts insects and other pests to your apartment complex.

Condominiums

Most condominium associations permit residents to keep hamsters and other small pets. If you live in a condo, check for specific restrictions before you acquire any new pets.

Owner Liability

The owner of a pet is responsible for any damage or injury the pet causes to persons or property. If a hamster belonging to you or your children should bite a person, you are liable. Therefore, it's a good idea to carry liability insurance; in addition, consider allowing only members of your family to handle the hamster.

Responsible Pet Owner

Be aware of the law in your municipality and keep your pets accordingly, so that neighbors will have no cause to complain. Also, stay informed, through pet-related organizations and your pet-owning friends, of impending local, state, and national legislation so you can support measures that protect the welfare of pets and enable you to retain your rights as a pet owner.

Some states have, or are considering, pet warranty and pet shop licensing laws, designed to protect the purchaser from unscrupulous practices and the animals from inhumane treatment. Other laws require animal breeders—even hobbyists—to pay licensing fees, obtain permits, and submit forms to state agencies. Some regulations limit the number of animals you may have on your property. If you plan to increase your household hamster population —and certainly if you plan to sell hamsters—you should inquire about such regulations.

Share Information

Your veterinarian, pet-owning friends, or a pet hobbyists' organization recommended by an experienced hamster breeder or established pet store owner can help you learn more about local, state, and national pet

legislation (see How to Learn More, page 125).

You can also:
✔ Monitor your local news and stay aware of issues which may affect pet owners.
✔ Present views of pet owners to your condominium or apartment board, friends, lawmakers, and the local media.
✔ Share your experiences and knowledge with government officials and your neighbors.
✔ If legislation is proposed that would limit the rights of pet owners, prepare a group of local pet enthusiasts to participate by speaking in support of keeping hamsters and other pets.
✔ Encourage other pet owners to become active in the legislative process, to advance legislation that will benefit all pet owners, and to support

legislation that strengthens anti-cruelty laws.

Positive Public Image

Your family can also promote a positive public image of pet owners and hamsters by participating in pet care programs sponsored by schools, scouting organizations, and other youth groups. Encourage your children to exhibit at state fairs, school events, hamster shows, and other animal-centered activities in your community.

For hamsters, acorns are a favorite souvenir from a walk outdoors.

Advice on Purchasing

When you go out to buy a hamster, you should allow plenty of time and not rely on the motto "Love at first sight." An exchange after the animal has already been brought home always leads to complications. To be totally pleased with your hamster it is especially important that the animal come from sound stock and be free of any physical defects (see chart on page 28).

How Do You Know a Good Pet Store When You See One?

It does make a difference where you buy your hamster. Just as you choose shops according to certain criteria for your own needs, you should be selective when you acquire a house pet. A good pet shop creates a favorable visual impression on the visitor.

■ The animals are located in a separate well-lighted roomy area.
■ Animals are displayed in nicely appointed cages that are not overcrowded and that provide the animals with comfortable living conditions until they are turned over to a new owner.

■ The cages in which animals are kept should be clean, with fresh bedding.
■ Food dishes and water bottles should be full.
■ No animals should be exhibited in the display window.
■ A good pet shop owner gladly takes time to discuss things and answer your questions thoroughly.

A reputable dealer will take pains to guide you to appro-

The purchase of a small, escape-proof transport cage is always worthwhile. The cage also serves as alternate quarters while the main cage is being cleaned.

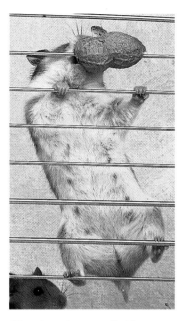

When hamsters are climbing, it's very easy to tell what sex they are. Here we see a female on the left and a male on the right.

Hamsters whose biorhythms have been permanently upset are susceptible to illnesses and may become fearful and aggressive.

You're better off not buying animals that are offered for sale in such an uncaring manner.

Hamster Preview

Buying a pet should never be an impulse purchase. Before visiting a pet store, it's a good idea to view the wide variety of hamsters from which you can choose, and to talk to as many experienced hamster owners as possible.

A Day's Outing

Contact the nearest exposition center or fairground to find out when the next pet exposition or state fair is being held. A day trip to one of these events presents an opportunity to learn about various animals, particularly the object of your search—hamsters. Hamster enthusiasts, breeders, and pet retailers display their best stock at pet expos. At fairs, hobbyists present hamsters they've lovingly raised and groomed in the hope of capturing a blue ribbon.

priate publications so you learn about hamster needs and behavior and avoid unpleasant experiences.

In many stores the hamsters are not provided with a house so that they can be seen by customers throughout the day. A conscientious pet store owner provides a house out of concern for the welfare of the animals.

If interior lighting in the store is left on at night, and hamsters, which become active at dusk, are subjected to glaring light, they experience stress and feel tormented.

Health Check at a Glance

	Healthy Hamster	**Sick Hamster**
Behavior	Daytime: sleeps peacefully Nighttime: lively, continually moving, sniffing everything, curious, outgoing	Daytime: sleep interrupted Nighttime: apathetic, lacking energy, not interested in surroundings, reserved
Overall Physical Appearance	Cylindrical body shape, well proportioned; straight back	Thin; sunken flanks; back bent upward
Skin	Pink, even, smooth, supple	Red, thickened, dry, scaly, crusty; with wounds or bald spots
Fur	Neat, shiny	Unkempt, matted
Eyes	Big, clear, black, protruding; tight-fitting eyelids	Sunken; opaque corneas; eyelids stuck together; discharge
Nose	Dry, clean	Sneezing, redness; mucous secretion, crustiness
Breathing	Effortless, regular, silent	Rattling, with open mouth
Mouth and Cheek Pouches	Dry, clean, odor free; cheek pouches are filled and emptied normally	Matted fur, salivating, redness sour or unpleasant odor; cheek pouches only slightly filled and emptied hesitantly or not at all
Anus and Genitals	Clean, dry, odor free	Matted fur, moist tail from diarrhea ("wet tail"), vaginal discharge
Extremities	Five toes on each foot, clean sole, balanced posture	Missing toes, soiled and inflamed soles, dragging an extremity, favoring one side in lying down

Hamsters like little between-meal snacks.

The Best Time of Day for Purchasing a Hamster

If hamsters are awakened during the day, they feel just as tired and grumpy as we humans do when we're disturbed in our nighttime sleep. They get angry (see Voice and Body Language, page 100), resist coming out of their warm nest, and even bite if you try to pull them out by force.

If you finally succeed in dragging them out of their house, they usually sniff around a little and then go back to their sleeping quarters. The same thing happens in a pet store when people want to buy a hamster during the day. The best time to buy a hamster is in the late afternoon near closing time.

Hamsters begin their evening activity between five and six o'clock; that's when they show their best side. Only at that time can you really see the little rodent's state of health and judge its freedom from externally visible flaws (see Health

Check at a Glance, page 28). While this "late-shift worker" has a big yawn, cleans up, and has a bite to eat, you can use the opportunity to check out cages, accessories, and feed. Be sure to check also on the prices of these items so that you can quickly verify that you've correctly figured out your finances. Remember, the hamster itself is reasonably priced, which is why you should always start with the accessories, and then buy the pet (see A Habitat for Hamsters, page 44).

How to Tell If a Hamster Is Healthy

In my veterinary practice I often wonder why some little hamsters are bought, or rather on what grounds a sick animal is chosen. "We felt so sorry for it," is frequently the answer. Added to that, ailing animals appear especially tame because of their poor health, and they create the impression that they are looking to the prospective purchaser for help. This pitiful demeanor is irresistible to many people, but it can be the start of a series of disappointments that often ends with putting the patient

to sleep. So never choose a hamster that doesn't appear to be entirely healthy.

Since hamsters, like all small rodents, are very robust and viable, you can conclude that young ones that have lost weight and are ostracized by the others are probably incurably ill. In such cases, reason must prevail over emotion. You have to check over the animal thoroughly and critically from head to toe. If you find a young hamster that has obvious symptoms of illness, report it to the pet shop owner. A responsible pet shop proprietor should be more than willing to take the necessary steps to care for the animal and provide veterinary care if necessary. After all, as long as an animal is in the pet shop, it belongs to the pet shop owner.

Hay and straw are popular materials for padding the sleeping nest. Chewing things up is one of the hamster's favorite activities.

The table on page 28 provides information on what a healthy hamster looks like, and what signs indicate that a hamster is sick.

Suggestion: If you identify an obviously sick animal among the hamsters offered for sale in the pet shop, you're probably better off not buying any hamsters from that group! You run the risk of choosing an animal that has already been infected and although it doesn't yet show any symptoms, will soon become sick. Taking a hamster out of the group and putting it into a new cage and a new environment is an additional source of stress that can instigate the outbreak of a dormant illness.

Noises that we can scarcely perceive and minute vibrations are part of the hamster's defensive behavior.

How to Tell a Hamster's Age

Because hamsters have a relatively short life expectancy of about two years, their age at purchase is quite important. Since it is not possible to determine precisely the age of an adult animal, it is recommended that only young hamsters be bought.

A young hamster three to four weeks old has attained half its body size—in the case of golden hamsters, about three to four inches (8 to 10 cm)—and is already completely independent. This weaning age, which coincides with an impressionable stage, is an ideal time for the animal to get used to humans.

Transportation Home

After purchase, it is standard practice to pack small rodents such as hamsters into folding boxes. Such boxes are also used for transporting pet birds to their new homes. If the trip home is short and if a second person can watch the box during the drive, using a folding box is fine.

But if the trip is longer, and if the box is not being watched by someone other than the driver of the car, there can be

31

some unpleasant surprises.

The air holes in the box give the hamster a place to begin chewing a larger opening. In a matter of seconds the hamster can gain freedom.

If you're lucky, you'll catch the nimble rodent before it disappears down into the car's upholstery. If not, there's no chance of apprehending the fugitive without taking the seat apart.

If you have to take the seat out, it's a good precautionary measure to do it in a closed garage so that the hamster doesn't disappear forever.

Hamsters can't escape from a special transport box for small rodents. So if it is at all possible, you should also buy that type of carrier (see photo, page 26).

You can get some reasonably priced plastic boxes measuring about 10 inches long by 6 inches wide by 7 inches high (25 cm × 15 cm × 18 cm) with a mesh floor and carrying handles. They are better than wire cages, because hamsters are very sensitive to cold, draft, and moisture.

Purchasing a transportation box is worthwhile for many reasons. It can also be used for

No exertion is too great to reach a couple of fresh beech leaves!

visits to the veterinarian and for temporary quarters while the main cage is being cleaned (see Taking Care of Cage and Accessories, page 70). Also it is easy to observe the hamster in such a box if, for example, it is injured and hides the second you try to get a good look at it. Hamsters divide their world up according to smells and recognize their home by its special scent. So take a little bedding or nesting material from the cage in the pet shop where the hamster has lived so far, and put it into the

A log with several holes drilled in it—even an artificial one made of plastic— stimulates the hamster's inquisitiveness.

transport container (see Observe, Learn, and Understand, page 94). The little fellow will then feel a little more at home. You should also be attentive to providing the familiar scent when you set up the hamster's new home.

Be Prepared

Experienced pet owners know that it's essential to be prepared before bringing a new animal home. Have a new cage ready, complete with clean bedding, full water bottle, and

toys from the pet store, so you can pop your new hamster right in. Put the familiar-smelling bedding from the pet store into the new cage right away, so your new pet will feel at home.

Suggestion: To encourage the little rodent to get used to you and become hand tamed as quickly as possible, don't demand too much of it at first. For more information on this, see the chapter entitled The Hamster in Its New Home, starting on page 102.

The Various Hamster Breeds

Years ago, when people went to pet shops to inquire about hamsters, they usually were shown a variegated golden hamster with typical golden-brown fur. In recent years, though, the selection has broadened significantly, and not all hamsters are alike.

The Zoological Classification System

Of the numerous naturally occurring hamster breeds there are essentially four types that are kept as house pets. These are usually not described and designated individually in pet shops or in pertinent literature.

In the zoological classification system hamsters are organized in the following ways:

Phylum: Muroides (*Muroidea*).
Order: Rodents (*Rodentia*).
Suborder: Myomorphs (*Myomorpha*).
Family: Burrowers (*Cricetidae*).
Genus: Hamster (*Cricetini*).
Species: medium hamster (*mesocretus*), gray dwarf hamster (*cricetulus*), short-tailed dwarf hamster (*phodopus*). The golden hamster (*mesocretus auratus*) belongs to the first species, the Chinese dwarf or striped hamster (*Cricetulus griseus*) belongs to the second, and the Djungarian dwarf hamsters (*Phodopus sungorus*) and the Roborowski dwarf hamster (*Phodopus roborovskii*) belong to the third.

The most important identifying features and characteristics of each breed are on the facing page.

The Syrian Golden Hamster

Mesocricetus auratus
By virtue of its size, the golden hamster belongs to the group known as the medium hamsters; it has a combined head and body length of 6 to 7 inches (15 to 18 cm) and a tail length of .5 inch (1.2 cm).

There are numerous variations that are distinguished by coloration, markings, hair structure, and essential features. That gives rise to the smoked hamster, for example, which has a

Smoked hamster. It's called that because its white base color darkens to a smoky tint on the nose, ears, tail, and paws.

Golden Hamster Breeds at a Glance

	Appearance	Features
Variegated golden hamster	Gold-colored back, white underside, dark ears, stocky build	Robust constitution, vital, aggressive with other hamsters, easy to tame, often moody
Cream-colored golden hamster	Head and back even beige color, underbelly somewhat lighter, dark ears, delicate build	Robust constitution, vital, peaceable with other hamsters, easy to tame, trouble-free
Smoked hamster	Head and back even white, dark markings on nose, ears, tail, and feet (acromelanin), dark red eyes, delicate build	Robust constitution, vital, peaceable with other hamsters, easy to tame, well adjusted
Plain golden hamster	Head and back even brown, gray, blue, black, sable, etc. Face and underbelly a bit lighter, various builds	Robust constitution, vital, relatively peaceable with other hamsters, easy to tame, sometimes moody
Dappled golden hamster	Dapples in form of white spots, sides, or stripes, in combination with all base colors, various builds	Less robust constitution, aggressive with other hamsters, difficult to tame, jumpy
Long-haired golden or angora hamster	Long, silky fur, in combination with all base colors and dapples, delicate build	Less robust and vital constitution, good natured with other hamsters, easy to tame, well adjusted
Teddy-golden or satin hamster	Plush fur, short- and long-haired in combination with most base colors, delicate build	Less robust and vital constitution, some variation in conduct toward other hamsters, very easy to tame, well adjusted
Rex golden hamster	Velvety fur which doesn't lie smooth, short-haired, in combination with some base colors, delicate build	Less robust and vital constitution, some variation in conduct toward other hamsters, easy to tame, well adjusted

short, even white coat, but with dark markings on the nose, ears, tail, and feet (see photo, page 34), or the long-haired golden hamster with its long silky coat (see photo, page 38).

One of the newest strains is the rex golden hamster. Its fur is short and velvety soft, but it doesn't lie smooth and flat. It comes in several base colors such as gray or blue.

For beginners the short-haired variegated and the plain golden hamster are recommended. These animals enjoy particularly robust health and are less sensitive than the other hamster breeds.

Note: A precise overview of the various types of golden hamsters and their different features is found in the chart on page 35.

Top: Dapples come in combination with all base colors.

Middle: Albinos are identifiable by their red eyes.

Left: Cream-colored golden hamster.

36

Top left: Black golden hamster.

Top right and below: The variegated golden hamster represents the typical form to which all variations are related.

The Chinese Dwarf or Striped Hamster
Cricetulus griseus

The Chinese dwarf or striped hamster is placed in the genus of the gray or long-tailed dwarf hamster (see Zoological Classification, page 34).

Its head and body measure from 3 to 4.75 inches in length (8 to 12 cm); its tail is .75 of an inch to a little over 1 inch long (2 to 3 cm). Its back is gray-brown in color, and it doesn't contrast markedly with the lighter underbelly. Most Chinese dwarf hamsters have a black stripe starting at the forehead and going down the middle of the back. The ears are very small, with a dark border. The slender body and pointed face, in contrast to that of other hamsters, are noteworthy (see photo, page 41).

Disposition: Chinese dwarf or striped hamsters still behave like wild animals. Females are extremely aggressive toward males. Only young animals can be tamed.

Djungarian Dwarf Hamsters
Phodopus sungorus

The Djungarian dwarf hamster is one of the short-tailed dwarf hamsters (see Zoological Classification System, page 34). Its head and body measure 2.75 to 4 inches in length (7 to 10 cm).

Top left: Cream-colored golden hamsters are especially distinctive.

Above right: Dappled teddy or satin hamster. Its plush, glistening silvery coat reminds people of teddy bears.

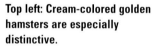

Left: Long-haired or angora hamsters are the only hamsters that need to be combed from time to time because of the nature of their coat.

Above left: Dappled hamsters like this black and white one are not always as easy to tame as hamsters of other colors.

Above right: The coat of the long-haired golden hamster can have a satiny sheen.

Right and below: Random dapples are most commonly offered for sale in pet shops.

39

Its little tail, which is only about .25 inch long (1 cm), doesn't even stick out of its fur. The gray-brown coloration of the back pushes into the white of the sides or the underbelly in three characteristic bulges. There is a narrow black stripe down the middle of the back.

In their natural surroundings Djungarian dwarf hamsters have a light gray, nearly white coat during the winter. A further distinguishing feature is the hair on the bottoms of their feet.

Disposition: Djungarian dwarf hamsters are extremely

Above left: Roborowski dwarf hamsters are recognizable by their tiny stature and the typical white spots over both eyes.

Above right: The Djungarian dwarf hamster has a nearly white coat during the winter.

The coloration on the back is a pale yellow with a trace of rust or gray. The underbelly and extremities are white. The bottoms of its feet, like those of the Djungarian dwarf hamster, are hairy. Two symmetrical white spots over the eyes are distinguishing features.

<u>Disposition:</u> Roborowski dwarf hamsters are very shy and rarely become hand tamed. Because of their small size, several can be put together in a large cage; a terrarium or cricetinarium (rodent cage) is best (see page 51).

Top: The Chinese dwarf or striped hamster belongs to the genus of long-tailed dwarf hamsters. Its tail, which is .75 inch to over 1 inch (2 to 3 cm) in length, is an identifying feature.

Right: Variegated long-haired or angora hamsters are more easygoing than their short-haired relatives.

Left: Even long-haired or angora hamsters can have dappled colors.

good-natured and peaceable.

<u>Disposition:</u> Several can be kept together in a sufficiently large cage or cricetinarium (see page 51).

The Roborowski Dwarf Hamster

Phodopus roborovskii
With a head and body measuring 2.75 to 3.5 inches (7 to 9 cm), this is the tiniest of the hamsters.

It too is classified in the genus of short-tailed dwarf hamsters (see Zoological Classification System, page 34).

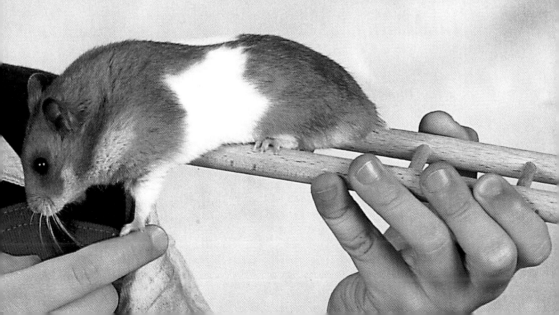

Proper Care and Handling

Hamsters are among the most appealing pets you can find. Once you understand their needs, it will be easy to provide living conditions to keep them healthy and happy.

A Habitat for Hamsters

The cage and its accessories are very important in keeping hamsters. They remain happy and fit only in a hamster house that corresponds to their needs.

A Place for the Cage

Before considering the purchase of a cage, you should decide where it will go.

A quiet place in the home is best, where the largely nocturnal hamster can sleep undisturbed through the day. In most cases, a quiet corner of the living room is appropriate for setting up the hamster cage. In nature, the hamster retires to its dark, nearly soundproof burrow deep under the surface after the night's exertions. Even the microclimate in the room where the cage is located is important for the hamster's happiness:

■ Temperature between 65°F and 80°F (18 to 26°C)

■ Humidity between 40 percent and 70 percent

■ Natural indirect daylight or moderate lighting
Above all, the temperature must not drop below the specified level, since golden hamsters shut down their metabolism and begin a type of hibernation at approximately 50°F. They can't survive temperatures below freezing, in contrast to dwarf hamsters, which remain active even at very cold temperatures. Also, excessive humidity condenses in the coat, making the hamster susceptible to upper respiratory infections.

Lighting should be moderate —about equal to the lighting in the hallway of a house. Inappropriate places include rooms where people smoke a lot or the television is constantly on. Also, continuous background noises from electrical appliances such as dishwashers or refrigerators are harmful to a hamster's health. Even floor vibrations from children romping around can detract from the deep sleep of the little rodents and shorten their life span.

The Right Type of Cage

Hamster cages come in a great variety of shapes, colors, and materials, and with different accessories. In buying a cage, you shouldn't just follow your esthetic sensibilities, but keep

TIP
▼
To afford your hamster a good view of its surroundings and a feeling of security, keep the cage on a small table or cabinet about 25 inches (65 cm) high. That also allows you to observe the hamster easily and enjoy its lively activity in the evening.

Golden hamsters like to climb—but only upwards. In the opposite direction, the climbing expedition often ends in a fall.

in mind the hamster's needs above all else.

Construction: In pet shops you can get good hamster cages in the form of plastic bottom pans with mesh inserts. The mesh inserts must fit in the bottom part in such a way that no chewable edges or rims stick into the interior of the cage. Otherwise, it won't take more than a couple of nights for the hamster to create an escape hatch.

Note: Hamsters are provided by nature with teeth that have an open root canal and grow continually. That's why hamsters gnaw on everything they can reach. So wooden cages for hamsters are out of the question. A further argument against wood construction is hygiene. Wood absorbs hamster urine, which is high in ammonia. The odor of ammonia not only disturbs our noses but also irritates the hamsters' mucous membranes. Because of their short legs, hamsters are continually forced to breath the air at floor level.

Bars: Bars must be placed horizontally so that the hamster can climb. Vertical bars provide no hold, and the hamster will slide off. To keep young hamsters from forcing their head between the bars, they should be no farther than .5 inch (12 mm) apart.

Dividing the hamster's cage into several levels increases floor space.

Bars and grates should have a dull chrome or galvanized finish. Colored finishes are no

A salt lick is a necessity (see page 68).

A water bottle with a spout belongs in every cage.

An exercise wheel provides opportunity for movement.

Healthy nibbling fun from the pet shop.

Dividing the hamster's cage into several levels increases floor space.

because only smooth surfaces can be cleaned effectively.

Access: The wire mesh should have several doors for the daily cage chores. There should be a door in the roof for taking the hamster out, and a door in the side for filling the food dish. There should also be a door in the front through which the hamster can climb when it's time to run around free. That door should be of a size that allows one end to be lowered to the floor at a moderate angle so that the hamster can use it as a ladder.

Depth of the cage bottom: An edge height of 3 to 4 inches (8 to 10 cm) is ideal. That way half the bedding won't get tossed out in the digging process, but the hamster can still see over the edge when it sits up.

Color of the cage bottom: Choose natural colors such as gray, brown, or green. Purple or pink won't harm the hamster, because it doesn't perceive colors; but natural colors are preferable for showing the hamster to its best advantage.

match for sharp teeth, and the wire underneath begins to rust. So avoid white or pink cages! Brass-type alloys are also unsuitable. Aside from the fact that such gratings reflect too much light for the sensitive hamster, as a result of gnawing and oxidation they quickly become unsightly. They also become unhygienic,

Cage size: A guideline for the minimum size is 24 inches long by 12 inches wide and 12 inches high (60 cm × 30 cm × 30 cm). There are no maximum limits; the more spacious the cage the better.

Cage shape: Rectangular shapes without ornamentation or other nonsense provide the best use of space.

Note: Round cages are not the best choice for hamsters. (See photo, page 114.) They tend to be very small (about 12 inches or 30 cm across), can scarcely be set up properly for hamsters, and are hard to bring into compliance with principles of proper animal care.

Also, the largely enclosed plastic units that are offered for sale are not recommended for hamsters. Apart from their small size, the individual pieces are often poorly designed, especially with respect to air exchange and heat buildup. In addition, hygiene will not be the best within the tube-shaped labyrinth-like passageways. The passageways need to be removed and cleaned with a bottle brush.

A house with a lid facilitates cleaning with the least amount of disruption to the arrangement for storing provisions set up by the hamster.

Food dishes must be stable. Their size should be such that the hamster can't climb into them.

An exercise wheel for hamsters must always be closed on the inside and allow easy entry from the outside.

Aquariums and Terrariums

Recessed aquariums and totally enclosed terrariums present some problems with regard to ventilation.

Because the hamster's excretions fall to the bottom of the cage, a high concentration of ammonia fumes settles to the bottom because the fumes are heavier than air. This leads to increased heat and humidity in the cage. Because of its tremendous activity, the hamster needs a large amount of oxygen. In conditions of inadequate air circulation, the resulting long-term stress leads to greater susceptibility to respiratory and skin infections. Glass cages and terrariums without side ventilation should cover an area of at least 32 by 16 inches and should not be higher than 14 inches (80 cm × 40 cm × 35 cm). But even those containers are not ideal. In order to satisfy their tremendous need to climb, hamsters continually wander back and forth along the glass, trying endlessly to jump up on it. In addition to the fact that these futile attempts to get out are frustrating and stressful for the hamster, the glass is always dirty and splattered with spittle.

Note: With glass cages hamsters often nibble on the glue that holds the panes together. In so doing, they may ingest substances that are harmful to their health.

Useful Accessories

Like all small rodents, hamsters like to travel through tunnels. Thanks to their powerful arm muscles, they can dig very well and climb with great dexterity. In the wild they are accustomed to leaving their burrow through a nearly vertical access that can be over 8 feet (2.5 m) long.

Therefore, they also need a properly constructed cage with fittings suited to hamsters.

Additional Levels

In order to increase the floor space of the cage, several levels can be set up. That is, of course, dependent upon having a cage that's high enough.

Additional floors made of plastic, with matching ramps, are available in pet shops. Plastic floors and ramps are easy to clean. They have raised edges and can be filled with shavings. However, since they don't stand up to hamster teeth for very long, they must be replaced from time to time. The cage can be divided into stories by small boards .25 inch to .63 inch (8 to 10 mm) thick placed crosswise. They can be connected by sticks (see Gnawing Material, page 68) or ladders. The boards can be held in place with screws that are attached to their

Hamsters like to sleep through the day in a completely enclosed hollow.

TIP

▼

It's not a good idea to put a hamster—not even the tiny Dwarf Hamster—in the kind of tank used as a terrarium or aquarium. It's better for your pet to put it in a cage. The glass walls of a tank prevent air from circulating, so the hamster does not get enough fresh air, and might become overheated.

Unfortunately, a whole apricot won't fit into the hamster's cheek pouches.

edges and that rest on the bars of the cage.

Note: Since the cost of the boards is minimal, it's a good idea for reasons of hygiene to make duplicate sets so you have a set of clean, dry boards in the cage while the other set is out for the weekly cleaning.

Sleeping Quarters— A Necessity

In the wild, hamsters sleep the day away in a nest at the end of their burrow. There it's consistently warm, dark, absolutely silent, and free of vibrations. Continuous, undisturbed sleep is vitally important to the little bundle of energy that's active for hours on end during the night. Hamsters that are not provided with the right accommodations for undisturbed sleep often become aggressive, sickly, and short-lived.

Pet shops offer sleeping houses of numerous designs for hamsters. They come in wood, plastic, and ceramic. They are placed on the bottom of the cage or are attached to the bars by means of hangers, and are accessible by ladders.

Wooden houses are usually square and very small. They are about 4 to 5 inches on a side and 3 to 4 inches high (10 to 12 cm × 8 to 10 cm). The doorway is about 1.5 inch (4 cm) across.

Plastic houses are about the same size. They look quite nice with their colored roofs and are easy to clean, but they have the disadvantage of getting steamed up with the moist breath of the hamster and becoming greasy. Also, it is not possible to take off and replace the roof without disturbing the sleeper.

Ceramic igloos (see photo, page 90) have the advantage of being impervious to gnawing. But they are too small for golden hamsters and too big for dwarf hamsters.

Note: When you buy a sleeping house make absolutely sure that it's big enough. You can tell a sleeping house is too

51

small if the hamster pushes it around the cage or even tips it over when it tries to enter with cheek pouches filled. In the interior there must be enough space for nesting material, for hamsters like to lie in a completely enclosed hollow (see photo, page 50). In addition, there must be room for the mandatory food storage that will be carried out every day. Such houses also must be dark enough, especially when the doorway and the useless little window are blocked off when the hamster goes to bed.

Skillful do-it-yourselfers can build a rectangular house that's suited to hamsters (see drawing, page 48). For that you use boards of .25 inch to .5 inch thick (5 to 10 cm) of spruce or pine. Chip board and plywood are unsuitable because the glue used in them is toxic to hamsters.

The pieces are screwed together or cemented with a nontoxic natural adhesive. The advantages of a homemade rectangular hamster house include stability, more darkness, more room for nesting material and collected food, less disruption in checking the nest, and more convenient cleaning.

How can you make your hamster happy?

Hamsters usually like big cages. These little animals need lots of exercise. Your hamster can really let off steam in a big cage with several stories. You can make your hamster particularly happy if you set up hiding places in the cage. Look at the picture on page 75. This cave consists of a piece of tree bark with moss on top. You can see how much the little hamster in the picture likes to slip under the bark and explore the "cave." You may be able to find a piece of bark in your yard or on a walk through the woods. If you can't find any bark, you can also use curved pieces of sheet cork, which is available in pet shops. For exercise outside the cage you should provide your hamster with a digging box. Hamsters dig enthusiastically with the help of their powerful front paws. For the digging box use a large, strong box such as a moving carton. Fill the bottom with about an 8-inch (20-cm) layer of bedding material for small animals. In the evening when your hamster is feeling its oats, take it out of its cage and put it into the digging box for an hour.

The ideal exercise wheel for hamsters is as large as possible, designed for safety, secure on its stand, quiet in operation, and impervious to gnawing.

Food Dishes

Strictly speaking, hamsters don't need food dishes, since they are accustomed to getting their food from the ground and cleaning it before collecting it in their cheek pouches. But you might want to purchase food dishes from the pet store for use inside the cage and to set them up as feeding places outside the cage for the hamster to find while it's running free (see page 58). If you do not use feeding bowls, especially for moist foods, unhygienic conditions may result. Even with dry food, a few kernels are usually left behind to get moldy.

Porcelain dishes or flat, enameled stoneware dishes are best suited (see drawing, page 48). They don't tip over and are easy to clean. They should be too small for the hamster to get into; otherwise, it will sit in the dish and soil the food with its excretions (see Taking Care of Hamsters, page 70).

Water

Although hamsters, as inhabitants of arid regions, meet their need for water by eating moist food, your pets should always have water available. Even if you almost never see them drink, you should not withhold water from them at any time, for any reason. Captive hamsters need a supplementary water source, especially in the summer. Water dishes quickly become soiled with bits of bedding, so you are better off using a water

bottle. Bottles with spouts work best. They are attached on the outside of the cage and the spout consists of an angled aluminum tube with a steel ball in the opening. When the hamster presses the ball upward with its lips or tongue, water drips out.

A recent nondrip innovation in water bottles is one with two steel balls, one behind the other.

Note: Glass bottles with no ball in the opening are adequate, but they tend to leak with fluctuating room temperatures. The result is soaked, smelly bedding.

Bedding

The right floor covering is important for the hamster's happiness. It should be absorbent and free of dust and harmful materials.

Small animal bedding, available at pet stores, is perfectly acceptable. It consists of dust-free wood shavings with no additives. Fill the bottom of the cage with the bedding to a depth of 1 to 2 inches.

Bark mulch and compressed straw, available in pet shops, are likewise recommended as bedding.

Gnawing provides necessary wear for the incisor teeth.

Sawdust and peat moss have too fine a texture. The dust created by digging irritates the hamster's eyelids and plugs up its nostrils. Breathing particles of moss, which often are musty, can produce life-threatening changes in lung tissues.

Cat litter is too dusty, and in the long run it's too abrasive on the hamster's foot pads.

Creature Comforts

Hamsters like to burrow deeply into their bedding to form a cozy sleeping cave. You'll add to your pet's comfort if you're generous with bedding to pad the cage floor. Spread natural cedar or pine chips over the bottom to a depth of one to two inches, and layer more bedding on top of that. Use extra bedding in the sleep area.

Your hamster will pile up some of the bedding to make a food storage area in one part of the cage. Here it will hoard the food it has stored in its pouches. It will use another section of bedding as a hamster toilet. You'll want to clean both of these areas frequently—every day or two

Hamsters occupy themselves with bunches of grain and grass as they would in the wild. Gnawing provides necessary wear for the incisor teeth.

—to prevent unpleasant odors and unhealthy conditions.

Nesting Material

Hamsters need nesting material to line and insulate their sleeping nests. They use it to build balls in the middle of which they can sleep all rolled up. Pet shops offer several different types.

<u>Lint</u> works very well as material for lining the nest. It consists of short linen threads and can be purchased in the pet shop.

<u>Synthetic cotton for hamsters</u> is less suitable, since it occasionally gets stuck in cheek pouches.

<u>Coconut fiber</u> like the product sold for nesting birds is too bulky, and it's easy for hamsters to cut their feet on it. You can get by without purchasing materials by

55

providing hay, straw, small twigs, wrapping paper, cellulose, unscented paper tissues, or toilet paper, for the hamster to gather up (see page 87).

Note: Wool and husk fibers can get wound around a hamster's feet and produce constrictions.

Hamster Toys and Exercise Wheel

Pet stores have several types of hamster toys for sale.

Wooden objects such as seesaws or hollowed-out cubes are appropriate. Note, however, that they are designed more for activity outside the cage. They take up too much room inside the cage.

Plastic gadgets are not suitable. Gnawed plastic splinters can produce severe digestive problems in hamsters.

An exercise wheel provides adequate movement, but uninterrupted running in the exercise wheel constitutes a kind of stereotypy (see page 112).

Hamsters are nocturnal, and like to run in their exercise wheel when humans like to be fast asleep, rather than lying awake in the dark listening to the repetitive squeaking of the wheel. When you purchase an exercise wheel, select one that you can attach securely in the cage, so it does not wobble. Be sure the wheel moves smoothly and soundlessly on its axle.

Note: Please also read the text on pages 115 to 117 on the subject of hamster toys or exercise wheels. Always consider the safety of your pet when you select toys.

A male hamster (right) is recognizable by its pointed tail end and its bulging, prominent testicles.

Hamster-proof Your House

Source of Danger	Possible Effect or Damage	Preventive Measures
Doors, windows	Escape, contusions, falls	Keep doors and windows closed during exercise periods
Ventilation ducts	Escape	Additional fine-mesh grating
Bases of built-in furniture, cracks in walls, radiators	Hiding, constructing a sleeping place, getting stuck, injuries	Close accesses, cover cabinets and radiators
Wood that is pressure-treated, painted, or treated with preservatives	Irritation of mucous membranes, symptoms of poisoning (salivating, diarrhea, labored breathing, cramps, unconsciousness), death	Use gates and keep fresh gnawing material available.
Electrical devices	Burns, shocks	Turn off electrical devices, avoid exposed wires, unplug, use child-proofing measures
Water dishes	Falling in, hypothermia, drowning	Remove or cover
Poisonous plants (see page 58), moldy potting soil	Poisoning symptoms (see above), death	Put up house plants, choose proper gnawing material
Medicine (tablets, pills)	Depending on active ingredients, signs of agitation, sleepiness, hypothermia	Keep containers closed; store in closed medicine cabinet
Textiles (rugs, curtains, knitting materials)	Use as nesting material, plugging up cheek pouches, poisoning, cutting with claws	Keep proper nesting material available, keep track of hamster while it's running free
Humans, dogs, cats	Injuries from getting stepped on, danger of being bitten or killed	While hamster is out of its cage, walk around, sit down, and lie down with care; keep other pets away

Running Free in the House

Allow only a fairly hand-tame adult hamster to run free. The room must be made "hamster proof" in preparation. Be sure to place out of reach all houseplants that are poisonous to hamsters. That includes, among others, primrose, holly, cacti, coralberry, belladonna, mistletoe, and poinsettia. Obtain a complete list of harmful plants from your veterinarian or library. Further sources of danger are detailed in the chart on page 57.

Outside the cage: Place the cage on the floor and open the front door. Let the hamster decide for itself when it wants to climb out. The floor should not be too slippery, cold, or drafty.

Don't allow yourself to be distracted while your hamster is running free. Keep track of where the animal is; otherwise, you might accidentally step on your pet.

You should set food out at certain places when your hamster is running free. That will motivate it to become active.

Sitting up with pads of front paws facing downward indicates heightened alertness.

Falling from a tabletop can produce fatal spinal column injuries. For that reason, when hamsters are allowed to run free they should always be at floor level. But even at floor level, there are countless dangers that the creatures don't recognize, chiefly because of their poor vision.

Note: Watch the hamster carefully while it's running around free. Place food and nesting material in various places around the room. That way the hamster is kept busy, as it is in the wild when it carries things back to the storage area or sleeping place.

<u>Back into the cage</u>: When the hamster gets hungry, it will usually go back into the cage on its own. If that takes too long, don't chase after it. That will only frighten the animal and immediately undermine its trust in you. It's better to set out treats such as dried fruit and try to lure it back into the cage. (See page 108.)

Note: Because of their diminutive size and nimbleness, dwarf hamsters are not eligible for outings in the home.

No Outdoor Exercise

It may be tempting to take the hamster out to the terrace and let it run around there or on the adjacent lawn, but that's a dangerous thing to do. It takes only minutes for animals to get their bearings in the new surroundings, and then their innate wild animal behavior takes over. In a flash, they discover a hiding place and are never found again. Even vertical walls present no obstacle to determined hamsters. They can easily climb on rough plaster. Loose soil motivates them to dig, and you find out very quickly what protective coloration is all about when they have disappeared into leaves or underbrush. A balcony or porch is inappropriate as a hamster exercise arena, unless you can afford to have it completely enclosed with jalousied windows or tight-fitting screens.

Proper Nutrition

Grain alone is not sufficient to keep your hamster healthy and fit. It needs some variety in its menu. Fresh fruits and vegetables, and protein-rich food, such as one to two mealworms or a teaspoon of cottage cheese every day, complete the nutrition list.

What Hamsters Eat in the Wild

As inhabitants of deserts and steppes, hamsters are not exactly gourmets. In order to survive, they must utilize everything edible that their environment offers them. Because the rainy season in their natural habitat is short, food availability varies greatly during the year. To adapt, hamsters are forced to economize on food supplies.

Hamsters have varied tastes, but they are predominantly vegetarians. Mostly they nibble blades of grass to get the seed-bearing tops. Next in order of preference are succulent foods such as leaves, stems, roots, and berries, all of

Stretching for food is a natural conditioning exercise.

which meet their need for fluid intake.

Supply animal protein, especially to growing young animals and nursing females. Live food items, such as mealworms, and small portions of meat, cheese, and yogurt are eagerly accepted.

The Art of Storing Supplies

The habit some rodents have of storing up provisions for use in hard times is well known and is reflected in some of our speech. We commonly speak of "squirreling away" large quantities of food for emergencies, for example. Hamsters, too, squirrel away foor by building chamber-like blind tunnels in their burrows, where they can store a six- to nine-month supply of food weighing many pounds.

Hamsters retain this innate drive even in their

cage; that is why they fill their cheek pouches with food or even a treat they've just been offered and take it into their sleeping house or into a hiding place in a corner of the cage. There it will be sorted and carefully piled up.

Hamsters will squirrel supplies away to the point at which they are forced to sleep outside their house because all the room is taken up by their collected provisions.

Therefore, on one hand the hamster house should not be too small, and on the other, food should be provided sparingly. Perishable fresh foods in particular should be restricted (see Basic Meal Plan, page 64).

Note: Hamster houses with a removable lid facilitate cleanup of rotting stored provisions, without destroying the hamster's organization of individual foods (see sketch, page 48).

Hamsters are very fond of cucumber slices. Leftover cucumbers rot quickly and need to be removed regularly from the hamster house.

Feeding Pet Hamsters

The hamster's nutritional requirements are as modest in the cage as in its original environment. It requires very little, and that little bit is usually not costly. Pet stores carry a wide variety of hamster feeds for every taste and pocketbook. The feed can be supplemented with green and moist food as well as animal protein.

But you shouldn't indiscriminately feed everything that comes to mind. The assertion that animals will eat only things that are good for them is not accurate.

Dry Food

This is the basis for hamsters' nutrition. It usually consists of ripe sunflower seeds, wheat, oats, corn, peas, pumpkin seeds, and compressed greens. Also, shelled peanuts, hazelnuts, walnuts, and bits of multi-colored cornmeal are added. To be adequate for all needs, a commercial hamster mix must contain all important nutrients and must guard against nutritional deficiencies. A nutritional analysis is on the packaging, as are guidelines for serving sizes and information on perishability. To cover all nutritional needs, the following ingredients must be included: 60 percent to 65 percent carbohydrate, 16 percent to 24 percent crude protein, 3 percent to 10 percent crude fat, 8 percent crude ash, crude fiber (cellulose and related substances), and water (moisture content). Natural food coloring may also be added.

If you gather greens for your hamster, you should learn what's good for it and what's not.

Shepherd's Purse

Dandelion

Ribwort

Raspberry

Rose Hips

Fresh green food, fruit, and vegetables provide nutrition.

Note: Don't buy food with only commonplace designations such as "Special Mixture," "High Quality Food," "Health Food," "Specifically Formulated Compound," or "Contains All Necessary Nutrients." Check the freshness date! If it's missing or illegible, let caution prevail. For safety, ask the sales people about perishability and check the smell and appearance of the food.

It must be neither dirty nor dusty, and it should not smell musty or rancid!

Moist Food

Fresh greens, fruit, and vegetables provide vitamins and minerals as well as the fluids that hamsters need. Greens can come from your yard, or, if you live in the country, you can bring them back from a walk. Favorites include dandelion, lady finger, shepherd's purse, ribwort, plantain, red and white clover, chickweed, sorrel, and sweet grasses (see drawings below). Carefully wash greens you've picked outdoors.

Note: Don't gather from the edge of the road or from freshly fertilized fields. In these places the greens are likely to have been subjected to auto fumes, road salt, fertilizers, and insecticides.

Fruit can be given in any form. Depending on the season, you can provide strawberries, raspberries, grapes, slices of apples and pears, as well as pitted cherries, plums, apricots, and peaches. Tropical fruits should be restricted to bananas, since citrus fruits with their relatively high citric acid content are not tolerated equally well by all animals (see Checklist of Symptoms of Illness, page 74).

People who want to feed dry fruits should buy them at a health food store and make sure they are not sulfurized.

Watercress Strawberry Parsley Peanut Pear

Basic Meal Plan for Proper Nutrition

Feeding Interval	Type of Food	Description and Quantity of Food*
Once a day	Dry food	Hamster mixture or complete feed in pellet form (one heaping tablespoonful or a little more than .5 ounce/15 g)
	Moist food	Fresh greens: five to ten herbs or grasses
		Fruits: one apple slice, one grape, or one strawberry
		Vegetables: one piece of carrot, one cucumber slice, one floret of cauliflower, or one lettuce leaf
	Live food	Mealworms: one to two
	Fiber	Hay and straw: one handful
	Gnawing material	Twigs: two to three
	Water	As much as the hamster wants (keep bottle filled)
Two to three times a week	Protein-rich food	Ground beef, cottage cheese, curds or fruit yogurt: one teaspoonful
Once a week	Treats	Crackers: one; dried fruits: one or two; dog biscuits: one

* Based on golden hamster; dwarf hamsters get half

Favorites include raisins, currants, apricots, dates, figs, plums, and rose hips.

Vegetables: You can give the hamster practically everything. In addition to the various leaf lettuces, spinach, chicory, parsley, and watercress, favorites include products with some "snap" like carrots, green beans, cucumbers, zucchini, broccoli, cauliflower, celery, red beets, tomatoes, and potatoes. The crunchy part of romaine is a welcome snack.

TIP

Treats should be served only sporadically. Don't be dazzled by the colorful packaging, and always read the nutrition label. Consider that the food must correspond to physical requirements if the animal is to avoid getting fat!

Protein-rich Food

Animal protein in modest quantities is an important part of hamster nutrition. Two to three helpings per week are sufficient. You can give ground beef, cottage cheese, or a favorite fruit yogurt.

Portions should be of a size that is consumed immediately, with no leftovers. The maximum for golden hamsters is one teaspoonful; for dwarf hamsters, half of that is enough. Anything that's left over will quickly turn into a clean-up problem because it spoils so quickly.

Dog biscuits are included in protein foods, too. Since they have a hard texture, they also serve as gnawing material.

Special Treats

Hamsters love that crunchy unsweetened oat cereal shaped like little Os. If you put a few pieces in its cage, your pet will gleefully stuff its pouches until you can see the outlines of the Os through its fur. Then it will scamper to its hoarding cave with its treasure.

Give treats only occasionally, because you don't want an overly hefty hamster whose already brief life span might be shortened by obesity (see Treats, page 67).

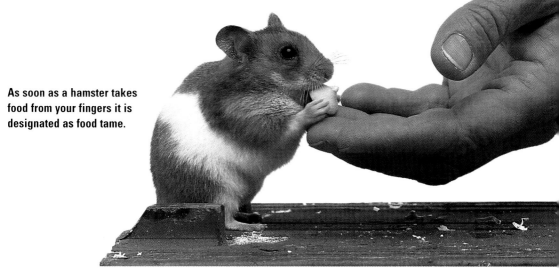

As soon as a hamster takes food from your fingers it is designated as food tame.

Live Food

Live foods from the pet store that are comparable to the small creatures that hamsters eat in the wild can be served from time to time. Crickets, grasshoppers, and mealworms are top choices. Mealworms are the larvae of the darkling beetle, and their advantage is that they can be stored for future use.

Keeping mealworms: Place the mealworms into a large glass jar that has been filled about halfway with oatmeal. Also place one or two washed and dried lettuce leaves into the jar. To avoid possibility of mold, it makes sense to clean the container at least once a week.

The more carefully the mealworms are cared for, the more food value they will have. The jar should be closed with a coarse cloth that lets air in (see photo on page 67). The jar should be kept in a place that's not too bright and at normal room temperature. You can give a hamster up to ten mealworms per week. Even the pupae and the darkling beetles that have just shed their skin will be consumed.

Crickets and grasshoppers

can be served from time to time; it's best to buy them fresh at the pet shop.

Fiber

Hamsters have no direct need for hay or straw, as rabbits do. But even with a substantial combination of foods, adding some fiber, or roughage, helps digestion.

The hay and straw provided for nesting material meets this purpose. Just be sure that they are of the best quality!

If you are reluctant to use your fingers to give your hamster mealworms, use tweezers.

Oatmeal and an occasional lettuce leaf are the basic foods of mealworms.

Should hamsters eat candy and chocolate?

Whenever Sandra wanted to give her hamster a treat, she would give it a piece of chocolate, a cookie, sweetened breakfast cereal, and sometimes a piece of candy. But the hamster became seriously ill from eating them. Its cheek pouches became plugged up and it couldn't eat any more. Sandra had to take her hamster to the veterinarian.

Sweets are not hamster food! Reward your hamster with some other kind of treat. For example, it will love one or two dried fruits such as raisins or dates, or you can give it a tea-spoonful of fruit yogurt. Be sure that it always has fresh twigs to gnaw on. That will make it very happy and keep its incisor teeth in shape.

Treats

In addition to dry feed mixtures, there are available in pet stores a number of prepared hamster treats that serve as food supplements. Designated as "Nibbles," "Crackers," and so forth, they indicate that, above all, their purpose is to provide the hamster with something on which to gnaw. Usually they are small pieces of wood fitted with a frame, to which sunflower seeds, dried fruits, and pieces of assorted nuts and grains are glued by means of molasses or honey.

The advantage of these commercial treats is that the animals are kept busy by gnawing, and the boredom of being in a cage is alleviated in a sensible way. The dis-advantage is the high fat content of these products; the crude fat content of nuts and sunflower seeds is around 50 percent. The same is true for the various fruit drops and tabs that keep appearing in the marketplace in new shapes.

Healthful Snacks

Your hamster's teeth are always growing, so you must keep it supplied with safe objects to gnaw, in order to keep its teeth the proper length for comfort and ease of eating.

Alfalfa squares, a fiber-rich treat that will keep your hamster's teeth in shape, are made of 100 percent dehydrated alfalfa. Your pet will enjoy gnawing the hard surfaces.

Ask your pet store manager about other hard treats that keep your hamster's teeth trim. The main advantage of these toothsome treats—at least to the hamster owner—is that, unlike lettuce and other moist

These nearly grown youngsters won't be tolerated by their mother much longer.

vegetable snacks, they don't turn to noisome mush, necessitating frequent cleaning of the hamster's hoarde.

Gnawing and Licking Material

Gnawing material in the form of fresh branches and twigs not only satisfies the need to gnaw and avoid boredom in the cage, but it also contains nutritionally valuable elements such as fat, starch, and minerals. The fiber or inner bark that lies beneath the outer bark seems to taste especially good. Chewing choices: Deciduous trees such as willow, beech, maple, birch, hazelnut, pear, and apple, with or without leaves, are good "chew toys" for hamsters. Twigs or branches of unknown wood or from ornamental bushes should not be used, since they often contain elements that are toxic to hamsters.

Note: Use no twigs from the side of the road (automobile emissions) or from sprayed fruit trees (insecticides)!

Salt Lick

Like all herbivores, hamsters have a need for additional salt. That's because a vegetarian diet has only about a tenth of the salt that is found in protein. You can recognize a salt deficiency when an animal licks all kinds of objects, even a person's skin.

Drinking Water

Opinions on the subject of drinking water for hamsters vary a great deal. That is because many of them are never seen drinking, or because they supply their need for fluids with their moist food. On the other hand, many hamsters can be observed repeatedly going to the water bottle throughout the night to quench their thirst. Since it is easy to provide water, and a lack of it can be harmful to the hamster's health, you should always provide fresh water for your hamster, even if you never see it use the bottle (see page 54). The most beneficial drink for small rodents is mineral water with no added carbonation. Tap water can be used only after it's been boiled, because of its high chlorine content, so most hamster owners rely instead on the convenience of commercial bottled water. Water should be changed every day.

Taking Care of Hamsters

Like all small rodents, golden hamsters are very conscious of cleanliness, and several times every day they groom themselves thoroughly. Taking care of hamsters, therefore, involves merely cleaning their cage and accessories.

Grooming

Hamsters lick their fur with their tongue and clean themselves with their front paws. Especially after sleeping, and after emptying their cheek pouches at the end of meals, hamsters give their fur a good going-over and make it shine. Hamsters should not be bathed, since they dry very slowly and catch cold easily.

Since the hamster takes such good care of its fur, combs and brushes are unnecessary. Only with long-haired golden hamsters or angora hamsters is it sometimes necessary to remove some pieces of bedding or nesting material that have become stuck to the fur.

Note: Excessively long claws, which occur only rarely, are a case for an expert. The veterinarian knows how to immobilize the hamster while its nails are being trimmed, and how much the claws can be shortened without causing them to bleed.

Taking Care of Cage and Accessories

Hamsters always establish one or two toilet areas in the cage, which they return to as needed. They keep the remainder of their cage meticulously clean.

Bedding needs changing entirely just once a week.

The corner used for urinating should be cleaned every two days. Remove the soaked bedding with a spatula reserved for that purpose.

Note: The sprays sold in pet shops to counteract the odor of hamster urine are useless; hamsters scarcely create an odor, and the sprays are an irritant to the animals.

The cage walls, mesh top, and accessories should be washed off with hot water once a week. Never use detergents or disinfectants.

The sleeping house must be cleaned regularly (see TIP, page 70). Remove only soiled nesting material so that as much as possible of the hamster's scent remains. Food dishes and water bottles need to be washed thoroughly every day with hot water.

T I P

▼

Spoiled leftovers from moist foods such as fruit and vegetables must regularly be removed from the sleeping house. You should leave the other provisions in the house, as much as possible in the order that the hamster created.

Hamsters spend a lot of time grooming their fur very thoroughly.

When you see sharp teeth cut through uncooked corn kernels, it's not surprising that a golden hamster can inflict a nasty bite.

There are special cleaning brushes for water bottles. The brushes are also used to prevent algae growth on glass containers.

The drinking spout with the two steel balls must also be cleaned.

A Daily Chore

Feeding a pet and keeping its cage clean are jobs that parents often assign to teach children responsibility. Too often, parents find it easier to do these jobs themselves, rather than constantly to remind children to do what they were told. As a parent, set aside time every day to help your child clean the cage. **Note:** During a major housecleaning, the hamster is best kept in a transportation container for small rodents (see photo, page 26).

71

Health Precautions and Illnesses

Hamsters naturally have a very robust constitution. With proper care and healthy nutrition, most animals will not become ill during their relatively short life span. If you have followed the advice given so far, you'll rarely have to seek the advice of a veterinarian.

Precaution Is Better Than Cure

■ Hamsters are extremely sensitive to stress.
When frightened or disturbed, they will react in much the same way humans do under the same circumstances—with increased cardiac activity, elevated blood pressure, added blood flow to skeletal muscles, and a release of blood sugar from the liver.

All these processes serve to provide the strength for a "fight or flight" response—to confront the enemy or to flee. A side effect is a weakening of the immune system and restricted blood flow to the skin, digestive system, and kidneys. That is why continued stress can cause skin diseases, digestive disorders, and kidney damage. In addition, stress interferes with metabolism and can lead to weight loss.

In particular, loud noises and disturbances during rest periods constitute an ongoing environment of stress for hamsters and reduce the body's resistance to illnesses (see A Place for the Cage, page 44).

Keeping incompatible animals together in too small a space with no place to get away from one another—so-called population pressure—also produces long-term stress (see One Hamster or Two?, page 18).

Toys like this polygon from the pet shop accommodate the hamster's need for activity.

Young hamsters have fun climbing together.

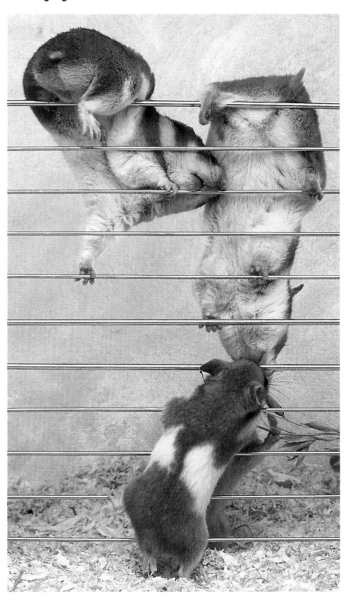

Such hamsters cut down their food intake, grow thin, are less active, neglect grooming, and become either depressed or aggressive.

Some causes of illness are:

■ Substantial fluctuations in temperature, lighting, and humidity (micro-climate) can trigger respiratory illnesses (see A Place for the Cage, page 44).

■ Imbalanced or spoiled food, poor drinking water, and pesticides and heavy metals in food plants also make hamsters susceptible to illnesses (see pages 63 and 68).

■ Life-threatening accidents most commonly occur while hamsters are running free in the house (see page 58) and in conjunction with exercise wheels (see page 114).

■ Filth in the cage can also impair a-hamster's health by increasing its susceptibility to infections (see pages 70–71).

Checklist of Symptoms of Illness

Observed Change	Causes That You Can Correct	Causes That Require Veterinary Care
Decreased activity, increased need to sleep, reduced food intake, weight loss	Too-low ambient temperature, long-standing stress (see page 72), problems with cage and furnishings lack of food, loneliness for partner	All illnesses involving general disorders such as infections and organ damage
Redness of skin, itching, scabs, hair loss	Dirty cage, heat build-up, excessive humidity, fights with other hamsters, inadequate nutrition	Skin parasites, fungus, extensive bite wounds, self-mutilation, hormonal disturbances
Runny eyes, aversion to light, swollen eyelids, sneezing, plugged nostrils, labored breathing with wheezing	Too-bright cage location, draft, dusty bedding, excessive or inadequate humidity, temperature fluctuations	Conjunctivitis, respiratory infection, incipient meningitis (LCM), inflammation of lungs
Matted fur around mouth, sour odor, wiping-motions across mouth, incomplete emptying of cheek pouches	Cheek pouches plugged with nesting material or stickiness from softened sweets	Dental anomalies, injuries and abscesses in cheek pouches
Shapeless, runny excrement with traces of blood, hunched back, foul odor, matted fur around anus and tail, rectal prolapse	Spoiled food, too much moist food, greens from roadside, toxic plants, unwashed fruit and vegetables, feeding directly from refrigerator	Inflammation of digestive system ("Wet Tail," see photo page 79), desiccation, weight loss
Limping, favoring a limb, dragging entire underside, wet fur on belly	Excessively long claws, cuts from improper nesting material, inadequate exercise wheel, too little organized exercise	Bite wounds, necrosis of foot from impaired circulation, sprains, fractures, spinal injuries

A hiding place like this one is a real treat for a hamster.

Symptoms of Illness

It's not easy to detect a hamster's illness early. The first things to notice are changes in your pet's living habits. If the hamster sleeps more than usual, acts listless, eats less, and wants to be left alone, these signs are an indication of trouble. Since such a small animal has limited reserves, and since it goes downhill very quickly because of its intense metabolism, the veterinarian should be contacted as soon as possible.

Note: The checklist on page 74 will help you to categorize properly any possible changes in your hamster.

The Most Common Illnesses

As already pointed out, most hamster illnesses are due to the way they are kept. Problems include accidental injuries, bite wounds, respiratory infections, digestive disorders with mild to severe diarrhea, and inflammatory changes in the surface of the body. By and large, hamster illnesses are not contagious to humans and pose no threat even to children. Illnesses that can be communicated from animal to human are designated as anthropozoonoses. Children have been known to contract infections from their hamster through intimate bodily contact such as cuddling, or as a result of inadequate cage cleanliness.

In proportion to the number of hamsters kept in houses, though, these illnesses are statistically insignificant. Just the same, you should be informed about the most important anthropozoonoses:

Lymphocytic Choriomeningitis (LCM)

One illness that concerned mothers often ask the veterinarian about is infectious meningitis. It is a viral infection that occurs in young hamsters up to the age of five months and that is communicable, especially in larger breeds.

<u>Symptoms</u>: Early manifestation can appear to be a cold with conjunctivitis and generally diminished well-being. In exceptional cases muscular cramps and paralysis sometimes occur.

Warning: This illness is communicable to humans. Infection occurs through urine, excrement, and saliva, and after an incubation period of one to two weeks it turns into flu-like symptoms with no further complications. There is, however, a more serious course the illness can take, which can lead to meningitis.

Climbing doesn't work so well from this side.

Occasionally a fresh ear of corn is a special treat for hamsters.

Most at risk are expectant mothers, in whom the virus can produce premature births and deformities in the fetus.

Treatment: If a young hamster becomes ill shortly after acquisition, you should always visit the veterinarian as a precaution. In case of doubt, LCM can be identified through blood tests. The disease is fatal to hamsters only in exceptional cases. Usually they get over it within three weeks.

Note: LCM infection occurs only in young hamsters. Older animals are not susceptible to the disease. When you buy a hamster, be sure to choose a healthy one (see page 28). You should also ask the salesperson in the pet shop if the hamster comes from a breeder that's free of LCM. Since the virus is not very hardy and quickly becomes passive outside the body, preventive hygienic measures add another degree of security (see page 70).

Salmonellosis

Salmonella is one of the most feared pathogens of digestive infections.

Symptoms: Diminished general well-being, rejection of food, and continuous diarrhea.

Cause: Infection with salmonella (*Salmonella typhimurium* and *Salmonella enteritidis*). Infection comes from food contaminated with excrement and from soiled bedding.

Treatment: Immediately consult a veterinarian. Salmonella infections usually lead to death in hamsters within a few days.

Attention: In order to rule out possible danger of infection to humans, a dead animal should be sent to a veterinary laboratory for examination. Salmonella can produce serious digestive disorders in children and adults. Your veterinarian will know where the appropriate diagnostic tests can be performed.

Trichophytosis

Trichophytosis is one of the most common fungal skin diseases.

Symptoms: At first, red blotches on the hamster's skin and severe itching. Later on, blisters and scabs, as well as round bald spots where hairs break off.

Cause: Contact with fungal spores (cause: *Trichophyton mentagrophytes*). Infection often occurs in hamsters through peat bedding. Animals with no visible change in skin condition also can transmit the fungus.

Treatment: Only by the veterinarian.

Notice: Children can easily pick up the fungus on their hands and face. Therefore, after handling a hamster they should wash their hands, and above all refrain from kissing hamsters! If itchy blotches appear on the skin, you must immediately consult a skin doctor.

The following are a few typical hamster illnesses that are relatively common, but which are not communicable to humans.

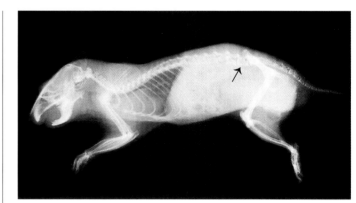

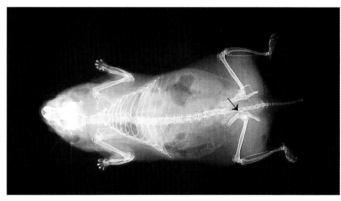

Wet Tail Sickness

Proliferative ileitis, or wet tail sickness, is observed especially in young hamsters from three to eight weeks old (see photo, opposite page, top).

Symptoms: Matted fur in anal region, loose diarrhea, prolapsed rectum (see photo, opposite page, bottom).

Causes: Various stressful causes, such as separation from

Even falls from modest heights can lead to serious injuries. In the X-ray at top, a fractured spine; below, a broken pelvis.

Wet tail disease is
often fatal.

Malignant tumor of
ear muscle (see page 80).

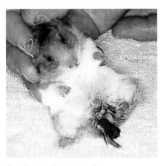

Prolapsed rectum in
a young hamster.

the mother, a new cage, transport, change in feed, and a too-cold cage location lead to a disturbance in intestinal bacteria, causing diarrhea.

Treatment: Immediately consult a veterinarian. In an acute case, animals die within two days. In nonacute cases that extend over several days, the veterinarian can help.

Note: Under no circumstances should you attempt to treat the pet with black tea, charcoal, or other home remedies. Every day without help from a veterinarian can mean the difference between life and death!

Salivary Illness

This involves inflammation of the salivary glands.

Symptoms: Similar to mumps.

Cause: Viral infection.

Treatment: Consult a veterinarian immediately. There is still no direct treatment available. But the veterinarian can resort to measures that enhance the body's defenses.

Mange Mite Infestation

An infestation of mange mites is among the most stubborn skin ailments.

Early symptoms: Damage to fur, reddened and scabby skin, itching.

Causes: Consult a veterinarian to determine whether the symptoms are caused by mange. The common types of mange are demodectic mange (cause: *Demodex criceti* and *Demodex aurati*), sarcoptic mange (cause: *Sarcoptes anacanthos*) and notoedric mange (cause: *Notoesdes notoedres*).

Treatment: Consult a veterinarian immediately. Since mange mites multiply almost exclusively in weakened animals with inadequate immune defenses, a treatment only for mange is usually not enough. Checking and improving overall conditions of how the animals are kept are requirements for successful therapy.

Cuts and Wounds

You can minimize serious bites and cuts by keeping hamsters in separate cages. If injury should occur, the hamster can usually hasten healing by licking its own wound. If the injury doesn't seem to be getting better, however, treat it with an antiseptic applied with a cotton swab. If the wound looks serious, take your pet to the veterinarian.

79

Keratoconjunctivitis

This illness is common to hamsters because of their button-like protruding eyes.

Symptoms: Pronounced tearing, which can be accompanied by drying of the surface of the eyes.

Causes: Dusty bedding, injuries in the vicinity of the eyes.

Treatment: Only by veterinarian. If treatment with appropriate eye preparations does not lead to recovery, or if the eyeball protrudes from the socket (exophthalmos), surgery to remove the damaged eye is unavoidable.

Tumors

Tumors are tissue growths that occur most often in older hamsters.

Symptoms: Swellings in the region of the teats and on the body surface.

Cause: The aging process in hamsters accelerates when they are about fifteen months old. From this point on, tumors can appear, and for the most part they are malignant.

Treatment: In this case, the veterinarian must decide if an operation is necessary. The size and location of the tumor, as well as the hamster's age, are decisive factors.

This worthwhile toy made of dried grass encourages the hamster's natural inquisitiveness.

How do you know that your hamster has grown old?

Hamsters live only two or three years. You'll recognize by its behavior and its appearance that your hamster is old, and that before long you'll have to deal with its death. In the evening, it no longer comes out of its house as energetically as before, but prefers to stay rolled up inside it. It "squirrels away" less food, and it is noticeably unsteady in its movements. Your hamster begins to lose weight, and its fur becomes unkempt. One day it lies dead in the cage. Try not to be too sad. A hamster simply can't live any longer, even if you have given it the very best care. If you enjoyed keeping your hamster, consider getting another one.

Taking Care of a Sick Hamster

Above all, a sick hamster needs quiet and warmth.

Heat lamps should always be directed on only part of the cage so that the animal can find a cooler spot. They must be placed at least two feet (60 cm) from the upper edge of the cage. You should carefully place a thermometer on top of the cage and make sure that the mercury does not climb above 85°F (30°C).

Areas around body orifices can be cleaned with a moistened cotton swab or with a special disposable wipe.

Note: Under no circumstances should you wash or bathe a hamster; otherwise, it may also catch a cold.

Medications are best given by means of a mealworm. Moisten or sprinkle it with the appropriate preparation and hold it with tweezers in front of the hamster's nose. If your hamster refuses to eat, ask your veterinarian how best to administer the medication.

Administering eye drops is something your veterinarian can show you how to do.

Taking the hamster's temperature is possible only with a thin thermal probe or a prismatic children's thermometer. Because of the danger of injury, taking a hamster's temperature is best left to the veterinarian.

False Alarm

Sometimes, after your hamster has stuffed its pouches almost to bursting, tears will dribble from its eyes, and it will sniffle. Before you assume it has a cold, examine its pouches. If excess food has accumulated, flush it out with warm water from a dropper.

Breeding Hamsters

Especially for children and adolescents, watching the mating, pregnancy, birth, and raising of young animals is a special experience, and it contributes to a better understanding of nature. But breeding hamsters also presents some problems.

The Problems of Breeding

Reproduction is an essential function of all life forms. Without offspring, a species soon becomes extinct. Like all animals, breeding is an essential element of hamster life in the wild. However, breeding of captive animals is not necessary for the survival of the species and is probably not appropriate for pet owners. The problem is that hamsters are among the most prolific mammals on earth. The female hamster brings an average of six to ten young into the world after an extremely short pregnancy of two weeks. Furthermore, in just one week, female hamsters are ready to breed again, and one pregnancy seems almost

A mother hamster with her young. The newborns come into the world completely naked and blind.

TIP

▼

For mating, always present the female to the male in the cage—not the other way around. Females are receptive to males every five or six days. On other days, they bite the males and drive them away to defend their territory.

In mating, the female hamster assumes a rigid posture.

to overlap another.

The short, trouble-free rearing of twenty-one days and the onset of sexual maturity at the age of three months favor meteoric reproduction. In the wild, hamsters must reproduce so prolifically because they have so many predators. Reproducing in large numbers is the only way they can ensure the survival of their kind.

Anyone who wants to obtain a pair of hamsters for breeding purposes should first find homes for the young animals. All too often an impulsive breeder is stuck with all or most of the young and is forced to buy additional cages, for week by week the animals become more quarrelsome. Furthermore, within a month's time the youngsters begin to take their turns at mating.

As we discussed earlier, people interested in getting a hamster want the animal they buy to be as young as possible. As hamsters grow older it becomes nearly impossible to find buyers for them. Four weeks pass by quickly, and the physical development of hamsters proceeds apace (see chart on page 91).

The pet shop where you bought your hamsters may be willing to sell the offspring. But first find out what the chances are of selling certain strains of golden hamsters or dwarf hamsters, so that you can decide in favor of one or the other.

Improve the Breed

The novice hamster owner should not attempt a breeding program without serious consideration and preparation. Reputable hobby breeders study genetics and keep careful records of which hamster is bred to which, in order to maintain and improve the health and characteristics of the breed.

And if you plan breeding as a profitable venture, forget it. There are far too many hamsters as it is, and you will probably end up giving them away.

Space Requirements

If you decide to breed your hamster, the first thing you need is a second cage, since males and females simply cannot tolerate one another when they are not breeding. To avoid injuries, which may prove fatal, males and females need to be kept far apart.

Only on the days when the female is in heat will she allow the male to approach her; her readiness to mate is communicated by a special scent (see page 99). By repeatedly placing the hamsters together you will find out if the female is ready and if they can be left

A mother grabs a wayward youngster and brings it back into the nest.

together, or if they still must be separated. In order to protect your hands, you should always wear leather gloves.

The cage in which they mate should be at least two feet long, one foot wide, and one foot deep (60 cm × 30 cm × 30 cm) in order to accommodate a second sleeping house. Later on the young will need the extra space.

Note: Breeding dwarf hamsters is easiest. The animals are so compatible that they may often be kept in pairs. Siblings that have never been separated are especially likely to get along well with one another. You merely need to be sure that they are of a proper age for breeding (see page 11).

If the little one is very fidgety, the mother grabs it in whatever way she can.

Mating Behavior

As soon as the female ceases to chase the male away, he begins the foreplay for mating.

The male nudges the female on the sides with his nose and licks her from head to tail. Then the genitals and under-belly undergo an intensive sniffing and examination.

The female pretends to run away a few steps. The male follows and tries repeatedly to push her hindquarters upward with his nose into the mating position. Suddenly the female assumes a rigid posture and stands with bent back and tail lifted vertically. Next comes the relatively short mating act, as the male rides the female (see photo, page 83). The rigidity is relaxed after coitus, and, following a thorough grooming, the whole ritual is repeated until the female rejects her partner.

Note: Whether you separate the two or leave them together depends on how they act. But at least with variegated golden hamsters love usually doesn't last longer than a day! The gentle breeds, such as the cream-colored hamster or the smoked hamster, may remain together for a longer period. The same is true for dwarf hamsters.

Gestation Period

The gestation period of hamsters is extremely short (see Gestation Period, page 11). After only a week, the increased food consumption, expanding abdomen, and behavior of the female show that conception has taken place. She is continually busy squirreling away food and nesting material in the house. This is when it's clearly advantageous to have a large sleeping house with removable lid (see drawing, page 48). If it is too small, the nest for the litter will be set up outside. This can create problems in nervous females (see Cannibalism, page 88).

If you want to check the nest, it is easy with a house that has a lid. Picking up a lidless house upsets the whole order when everything inside slides around (see Checking the Nest, page 87).

You can contribute very little for the benefit of the expectant mother hamster. But make note of the following:

What is Michael going to do with all these hamsters?

Mark owns a breeding pair of golden hamsters. Since the two animals can't coexist peacefully, he gives the female to his friend Michael. One morning when Michael peers into the cage, he can't believe his eyes. Six naked baby hamsters lie in the nest. That's why the golden hamster couple had gotten along so well for a short time. The young ones were the sudden proof. But what was Michael going to do with all the hamsters? He realized that the young would be nearly grown in just three weeks. Then there would be discord in the cage; the mother hamster would no longer tolerate the little ones in her presence. So the young would have to be separated from the mother. In addition, as soon as the young females reached eight weeks of age, they too would be able to have babies. Four of the six young were females. Michael calculated quickly: If each of the females had six young he would soon have thirty hamsters! Michael immediately sat down at his desk and wrote a notice for the bulletin board at his school: "Six baby hamsters free for the taking." Thank goodness Michael found classmates to take the little hamsters off his hands.

T I P

▼

The pregnant female hamster eagerly brings nesting material into the sleeping house. For her free exercise around the room, you should set out pieces of wrapping paper, cellulose, toilet paper, and a little hay or straw. That keeps the animal busy transporting things to the nest, just as hamsters do in the wild.

When you buy a hamster, you should always be sure to get a young one.

■ Try to preserve quiet; avoid noise and vibrations.

■ Change nothing in the vicinity of the cage.

■ Have available adequate lint, hay, straw, and wrapping paper for making the nest.

■ Take into account increased need for food; double protein and moist food rations.

■ Change the bedding two days before due date and then disturb the nest no more (you don't want to change the scent).

Birth

Usually the little hamsters are born without complication during the night. If perchance you are there for the birth, don't watch and don't try to help. Mother hamsters react very sensitively to every kind of disturbance. They can abandon the nest and carry the newborn babies in their cheek pouches to some other place in the cage and leave them there or even eat them (see page 88).

Birth takes about half an hour. The hamster shows little distress as the young are born in short intervals one after another. The mother uses her incisors to tear off the amniotic sack, and she eats it along with the afterbirth. Finally she bites off the umbilical cord and licks the young dry. A short while later, the newborns suckle for the first time.

Checking the Nest

In the first days after the birth, the mother scarcely leaves the nest, since she must provide warmth for her completely naked young.

87

In the first days they remain under her, attached firmly to her teats. If the cage appears orderly and nothing is stirring except for a soft peeping from the direction of the sleeping house, you can conclude that all's fine with the offspring.

Note: Just the same, look into the nest every day to see that everything is as it should be. It's best to wait until the female hamster has left the house, or to lure her out with a treat. Don't check the nest while she's inside, because that's a major disruption.

It can also happen that the mother hamster's protective instinct is so strong that she goes back into the house as soon as anything stirs. That's why you need to be quick and lift the lid for just a brief moment. If the young are covered up, push the nesting material aside with a stick from the cage—but never with the finger, since its scent is alien to the mother hamster.

If you find a dead young one in the nest, remove it with tweezers. When you're finished, turn the bedding back down.

Cannibalism

When the mother eats its young, the behavior is known as cannibalism. In the wild, hamsters resort to cannibalism when there are too many animals of the same type living in too restricted an area—in other words, under conditions of overcrowding.

This behavior is often observed among many small mammals after cage births. The causes can be quite varied:

<u>Disturbances in the surroundings</u>: Nervous mother hamsters may react to disturbances during birth and to scent changes in the nest by eating their young. Since even at later periods throughout the nursing phase strange scents are perceived as irritants, cleaning measures must be suspended during this time (see Checking the Nest, page 88).

<u>Lack of restraining cry</u>: When the mother eats the umbilical cord, a healthy baby will emit a cry as soon as the navel opening is reached.

This restraining cry causes the mother to stop eating.

But if that acoustical warning signal is absent because the little one is very weak or dead, the mother hamster simply keeps eating.

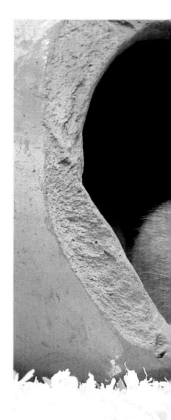

Only young hamsters get along with one another. They turn into loners as soon as they are grown.

Lack of protein: Females that have been bred very early, before they are fully developed adults, and mothers that become pregnant immediately after giving birth, can experience a protein deficiency. This lack may be offset by eating the young.

Disruption of milk production: If the mother has too little milk, which can be caused by continual stress, she may resort to cannibalizing her young.

Population pressure: If the cage is too heavily populated, hamsters temporarily cease producing scent in their glands. As a result, the young are no longer scent marked and are, therefore, unrecognizable by the mother; that leads to cannibalism.

Raising Young Hamsters

Female hamsters are conscientious mothers who take caring for their young very seriously.

As typical long-term nesters, young hamsters are totally dependent on the mother. The mother stays continually with them in the first days after birth, except for short breaks. In addition to warming and suckling, her main task consists of cleaning their bodily orifices by removing any droppings or urine. She prompts their digestion by intensively licking them on the belly. She also sees to it that none of the youngsters get too far away from the protection of the nest. As soon as she hears the appropriate emergency cry (see Hearing, page 96), she seizes the runaway by the nape of the neck and hauls it back to the nest. The same thing happens when a youngster has clamped tightly onto the mother's teat and is dragged out of the nest when she steps out.

For the most part, the development of the young outside the mother proceeds with almost the same speed as during pregnancy (see chart, page 91).

You'll probably want to keep the best babies and send the others to new homes, which you've already picked out before your hamster was bred. It's not easy to assess baby hamsters. Newborns—all pink skin and scrawny legs— are not at all attractive. When their coat starts to develop its color and texture, ask an experienced breeder if you have quality stock. If not, and you would like to become a breeder, invest in excellent breeding stock and several books on genetics.

A clay igloo lined with lint is an ideal sleeping place for dwarf hamsters.

Biogram of Physical Development

First Day	Hairless and reddish skin Eyes closed Limbs weak and underdeveloped Uncoordinated movements Elimination of droppings and urine by means of belly massage by mother
Second Day	Skin pigmentation begins
Fifth Day	Hair begins to grow First solid food Inception of grooming movements
Tenth Day	Eyes open Filling and emptying cheek pouches Grooming Elimination of droppings and urine without mother's help
Fourteenth Day	Leaving nest Playing with siblings
Twenty-first Day	Complete independence

Removing the Young Hamsters

At three weeks old, the young hamsters are independent. Now, of all times, when the young are the nicest and you can't get enough of their play fighting, they have to be given away.

By the time they are six weeks of age, the animals will be fully grown and scarcely compatible any more.

So call the pet store or people you know who want a hamster, and tell them that the little ones are ready to be picked up. If their adoption is delayed for one reason or another, the young must be separated from the mother. The young themselves can stay together for another month. After that, they must be placed in separate cages.

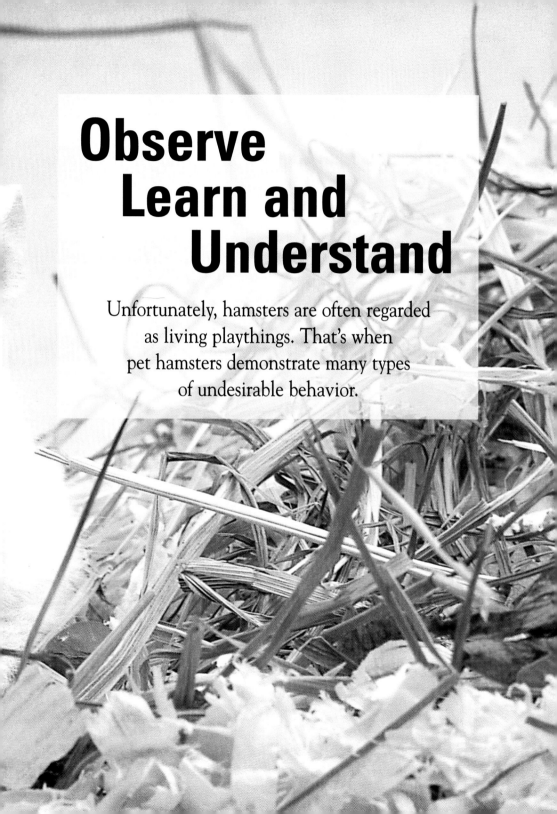

Observe Learn and Understand

Unfortunately, hamsters are often regarded as living playthings. That's when pet hamsters demonstrate many types of undesirable behavior.

What Hamsters Can Do

In order to understand your hamster and give it proper time and attention, you have to know something about its biology and its physical features. It's also important to have a correct understanding of its body language and vocal signals.

Behavior in the Wild

Captive hamsters have scarcely modified their natural behavior even though they have been living under the care of humans for many generations (see Hamsters Are Still Wild Animals, page 12).

When darkness falls upon the hamster's natural habitat in the desert or the steppes, the small rodents emerge from their hiding places and devote themselves to searching for food. The hustle and bustle of food gathering allows them to carry out their tremendous daily quota of running, because vegetation in the desert or steppes is very sparse. Mostly they snip off seed-bearing grass stems with their sharp teeth to reach the

By providing fresh gnawing material, you can meet the hamster's need to use its incisor teeth.

TIP

▼

If the cage is placed in a location that's too cold, with a room temperature under 59°F (15°C), even a caged hamster can undergo a type of hibernation. So if it suddenly diminishes its accustomed liveliness, don't automatically suspect a mysterious illness, but rather a defective radiator!

A hamster's conception of the Land of Milk and Honey.

nutritious seed clusters.

Except for a few small things that they eat right away, they gather up everything edible in their cheek pouches and transport it to their burrow. There everything is sorted according to food type and stored away. This "squirreling away" assures food availability in colder times.

The burrow can be as deep as 2.5 yards (2 m) under the earth and is reached through a tunnel that goes down almost vertically.

When the outside temperature dips below 59°F (15°C), the animals' activity begins to slacken noticeably. With the onset of the first cold weather the hamster plugs up its burrow and slips into a hibernation that lasts until the weather becomes warmer. Its body temperature

sinks to a level just above the surrounding temperature, and breathing and heart rate are reduced to a minimum. Since it breathes only once per minute instead of a hundred times, and its heart beats only four times per minute rather than five hundred, it acts in this state as if it were dead. The hamster briefly interrupts its rest once a week to eat a little of the food it stored in the burrow during the warmer months

The Hamster's Senses

Vision: As a creature of the night, the hamster has no use for acute vision. It doesn't see colors and forms very clearly. On the other hand, its round eyes on the sides of its head can take in its entire surroundings with a single glance. By our standards, it is quite near-sighted, since it can scarcely see shapes clearly more than a yard away. Movements such as those of an enemy, however, are perceived from a greater distance. In daylight the hamster is nearly blind. That explains its frequently observed fear when it suddenly enters unfamiliar surroundings. Even its susceptibility to falling is connected to the inadequacy of its depth perception in bright light (see Running Free in the House, page 58).

Hearing: The hamster's hearing is very highly developed; it can perceive ultrasonic frequencies beyond the normal range of human hearing. This is important for not only protection from enemies, but also communication with other hamsters. It's known that baby hamsters can use sounds inaudible to other animals to call their mother if it gets too cold in the nest without her, or if they are hungry and want to suckle. It also seems that hamsters can differentiate among voices and recognize their caregivers after a while if, for example, the people always use the same

words of greeting. In order to sleep undisturbed through the day, hamsters fold their ear muscles together.

Smell: Hamsters get their bearings primarily through the sense of smell. They smell food

A handful of fragrant hay in the cage turns into an adventure for hamsters.

Hamsters are especially fond of juicy melon. Here's a real family-size portion.

In grooming, no spot on the body is left out.

The hamster in the foreground is yawning widely. This communicates a sense of well-being.

Complete relaxation. Hamsters like to be warm and snug when they sleep.

from great distances. By means of droppings and urine, as well as scent markings, which they constantly deposit from sebaceous glands on both sides of their body, they easily find their area in the darkness and simultaneously notify intruders of their claim to the territory. Dwarf hamsters have sebaceous glands, known as ventral glands, on the underside of their body.

Just as we visually take note of a person's appearance, hamsters accumulate scent portraits and use them to recognize other hamsters, enemies, and even people. Courting couples or extended family members recognize each other by the group scent, which determines aggressive or peaceful behavior.

Note: If a hamster is put into unfamiliar surroundings or is handled by a person unknown to the group, the group scent can be changed so permanently that hostilities and injuries from biting may result. So under no circumstances should strange animals be placed together.

Touch: Tactile hairs (vibrissa) on the face, on the sides of the body, and on the extremities help hamsters to navigate through terrain at night, to perceive obstacles in their way. The tactile hairs that jut out from both sides of the face also help in evaluating if the opening of a hole or a hiding place is large enough to enter.

Anatomical Features

Cheek pouches: Particularly noticeable on hamsters are their cheek pouches, which can extend from the cleavage in the lip to the far side of the head beneath the ear. The pouches are lined with a dry, tough, bristly skin. The bristles keep the food secure and keep it from falling out or slipping into the oral cavity. To empty the pouches, hamsters press the contents toward the oral cavity with the front paws and knead them out.

Digestive processes such as salivating on the food do not take place in the cheek pouches, so the food coming out of the cheek pouches looks pretty much like it did before the hamster gathered it.

Teeth: The hamster's mouth contains sixteen teeth—four incisors and eight molars. Its incisors, which are used for gnawing, have an open root canal and grow continually throughout its life. If gnawing

97

material is not available to grind the teeth down, the hamster will no longer be able to close its mouth properly. If this happens your veterinarian will have to trim your pet's teeth. To avoid frequent visits to the veterinarian, choose your hamster only from well-bred stock. Keep it supplied with toys and snacks it can gnaw to keep its teeth trimmed. On each of the four molars of the upper and lower jaw there are two rows of small chewing protuberances for grinding food. Problems with molars occur less often then with incisors because the movement of the lower jaw usually causes sufficient grinding of the molar surfaces against each other.

Stomach and intestines: Hamsters have a rumen for softening the food and a glandular stomach where food is broken down with the help of enzymes.

As with all small rodents, the intestinal bacteria of hamsters are very sensitive to medications containing antibiotics.

Note: Never give the animal any antibiotic on a hunch, just because it has worked on you or your children. That could prove fatal to the hamster.

Forelegs: The extremely powerful forelegs of hamsters are used for more than grasping food; they are also useful in digging and climbing.

The forepaws have four toes and a rudimentary thumb; the hind paws have five completely developed toes. On level ground, hamsters can move quickly with ease.

It is a dangerous situation when a hamster climbs up on something and is not in a position to climb back down. Hamsters readily let themselves fall—in the wild landing on soft sand is not a problem, but a fall to a hard floor from the height of a table can produce fatal injuries such as spinal or pelvic fractures (see photos on page 78).

Hamsters have a very delicate and fracture-prone skeleton that is out of proportion to their body mass. Their legs are too short to absorb the impact of a fall.

The Whole Picture

If all the elements of the hamster's anatomy fit together as they should, the animal is considered to have proper conformation. This quality is not only desirable to breeders and to judges at hamster

TIP

▼

If your hamster puts no weight on one limb or drags it while running, you must consider the possibility that it fell and broke a bone. Immediately visit the veterinarian with the little patient. Only in the rarest of cases are you dealing with a harmless contusion. Hamsters take pain well and may even run in their exercise wheel in spite of a broken lower leg.

Young hamsters need to learn how to use the exercise wheel properly.

shows, but also indicative of a healthy individual that will be a long-lived pet.

The Hamster's Social Behavior

In their social behavior, hamsters prefer to be alone, and golden hamsters are particularly intolerant of other hamsters. Only at mating time will a female tolerate a male in her vicinity. Females indicate receptiveness to mating or rejection of the partner by means of a specific scent. At all other times, intruding males that choose not to comply with the directive to leave are driven away by biting. A mother tolerates her young through the end of the rearing phase of about twenty-one days. Then they too are banished.

Voice and Body Language

Hamster behavior is motivated chiefly by territorial defense. As a result, their body and voice language are not as distinctive as those of other small mammals that live in lasting partnerships or in bands. So you shouldn't expect any particular social behavior or greeting rituals from your hamster.

Hamster body language can be explained as follows:

■ Placing the nose on the ground over and over in quick succession = food search, hunger.

■ Crawling along on the ground and using anything available for cover = insecurity resulting from unfamiliar surroundings.

■ Sudden pauses, hectic grooming = perplexity, excitement (see drawing, page 101).

■ Stilted gait with raised hindquarters and erect tail = submission to a stronger animal—usually observed when young hamsters defer to older ones.

■ Rising up on hind legs, upper body leaning slightly toward front, nose high, ears raised, pads of forepaws pointing downward = curiosity, protection (see drawing, page 100).

Top: Defense, but also readiness to fight.

Bottom: Protective posture (left), defensive stance (right).

Top: Hectic grooming indicates perplexity.

Bottom: Stretching and yawning are signs of happiness.

■ Rising on hindquarters, upper body somewhat inclined to the rear, baring incisors, ears laid back, pads of forepaws turning upward = warning, aggression (see drawing, page 100).

■ Lying entirely on back, inflating cheek pouches, remaining silent and motionless, ears laid back, pads of all four paws pointing upward = defense, readiness to fight (see drawing, page 100).

■ Continuous, thorough grooming = coziness, feeling of comfort.

■ Stretching and yawning = peace, balance, happiness (see drawing below left).

■ Jumping into the air = high spirits, especially evident in young hamsters during "jumping phase."

The hamster's voice is used more for confrontation than for small talk:

■ Growling = ill humor, aggression.

■ Hissing = defense, threat.

■ Gnashing teeth = warning, aggression, demonstration of biting ability.

■ Squeaking = sound that accompanies biting.

■ Squealing = pain, fear, anxiety.

The Hamster in Its New Home

In helping your new housemate get settled in, you must proceed very gently. How quickly the hamster adjusts to its new environment and becomes confident and hand tamed depends on your sensitivity.

The First Hours

In daylight, hamsters can hardly see anything and only at dusk come into their own, so you should put off the gala reception to the new home until evening (see The Best Time of Day for Purchasing a Hamster, page 29).

The new surroundings are a terrain as alien for the hamster as a new dwelling is for us, where we have to find the light switches, water meter, and trash cans.

Above all, the strange scents present problems and must be processed through intensive sniffing (see Smell, page 96).

The entrance to the sleeping house, the ladder to the next level in the cage, and the diameter of the exercise wheel must be explored with the tactile hairs and their size filed away for navigating in the dark. The hamster also must get used to new sounds in the environment and different lighting conditions.

Children especially must be patient in spite of their excitement and curiosity to find out what the new housemate will do.

Under no circumstances should a flashlight be shone into the cage, or should a stick inserted between the bars be used to guide the hamster to the exercise wheel or food dish. The hamster's sure to find the way to the second floor and to the drinks all by itself, so don't force it in any direction or nudge it along.

If you want to make your hamster happy and help it settle in easily, you should give it some of the familiar food, nesting material, and bedding from its previous cage in the pet store (see Transportation Home, page 31). The sooner it smells familiar scents, the more quickly it will lose its shyness and the sooner it will feel comfortable. A quiet location, reduced light, a warm and comfortable temperature, and protection from view by the partial covering of a cloth over the cage will help the hamster feel at home more quickly.

T I P

In the first days in its new home, the hamster should be left alone as much as possible. That's especially hard for children to do. That's why it's important to explain the hamster's behavior to a child. The advice given here will help you create the proper understanding.

Hamsters are essentially pets for watching. They are not for cuddling and snuggling.

The First Days

For the first few days, leave the newcomer alone and don't expect too much of it.

Above all, during the day you must strictly restrain your curiosity and your concern for its well-being and refrain from interrupting its sleep (see Sleeping Quarters, page 51).

For the first few days, limit your activity near the hamster. Move around quietly near its cage. Talk and sing softly so it will become accustomed to your voice. Be careful not to jar the cage when you offer food or water, or reach in to change urine-soaked bedding or to remove moist vegetables on the verge of decay. As you do this, speak in low, reassuring tones so the new pet will not be alarmed. Wear gardening gloves at first to protect your hands, because if the hamster becomes upset at your approach, it might panic and attempt to bite in self-defense. **Note:** At first, only fill the food dish and renew the drinking water every day. Aside from that, all tasks involving the cage should cease, and the

chosen cage location should not be changed.

The first phase of adjustment is over as soon as the hamster stops its hectic bustling around, repeatedly yawns heartily and stretches, and grooms its coat thoroughly (see Body Language, pages 100–101). That's how it expresses its feeling that the world is pretty much in order. Now you can think about making contact slowly by hand (see Food Tame, Finger Tame, Hand Tame, page 106). The first exercise sessions outside the cage can now take place (see Running Free in the House, page 58).

The Hamster and Other House Pets

Many people like the idea of letting the hamster run around in the house with other animals. This idea must be rejected right away! Hamsters are such incorrigible loners that they place no value on society. They regard not only other hamsters, but also all other small rodents, as enemy intruders in their territory. Mice, gerbils, and chipmunks have a scent unlike that of the hamster. Before long, serious biting will result.

Rabbits and guinea pigs are distinctly peace-loving animals, but even here there is danger if they are placed with hamsters. Since rabbits and guinea pigs are larger than hamsters, a hamster can be easily injured. Large birds such as most parrots can cause hamsters serious injury with their strong beaks. Small birds such as parakeets, parrotlets, finches, and canaries may peck at the hamster if it approaches the bars of their cages. Small frogs, lizards and other amphibians and reptiles might awaken the hamster's hunting instinct.

Large lizards and snakes, on the other hand, might regard as lunch a hamster trespassing in their territory. If you've handled other small pets,

Hungry no more! The cracker will be taken into the house and stored for future use.

If you want to paint your hamster's house, use only nontoxic paints.

wash your hands before you pick up your hamster. The scent of other mammals might excite your pet into biting you. With dogs and cats, hamsters normally trigger the hunting instinct and are considered prey. Of course, there are always exceptions, and such animals sometimes get used to one another. But I can only advise against experiments in this vein.

Note: Don't try to force the hamster to socialize. Even if it tolerates another pet contrary to expectations, you should be prepared for a sudden change of heart.

Fun and Games With Your Hamster

Arrange a branch and apple slices to make an apple tree for your hamster.

Hamsters are not pets for cuddling or petting; rather, they are for people who enjoy watching their antics. Still, it is possible to hand tame them, and there are activities you can enjoy with them.

Food Taming—Finger Taming—Hand Taming

Food taming: The hamster gathers its first information about you by sniffing your hand. That is why it's important for you to smell friendly at your first meeting, in order to inspire as much confidence as possible.

With hamsters, this is accomplished not with perfumes, but by rubbing some of its moist bedding between your hands before you hold a finger in front of its nose for examination. If you are lucky, it will accept the offer and climb right onto your hand, especially if the hamster has already been hand tamed. But usually young hamsters are rather shy, and you have to find another way to establish contact.

It's best to begin by holding

treats between thumb and forefinger and offering them through the bars of the cage. Good choices are pear or apple slices or tasty mealworms. Once the hamster has come to accept these offerings, hold onto the next tidbit a little longer so that the animal has to stay at your hand longer. Later, repeat the process with the top off the cage. As soon as this hand feeding is successful, the hamster has earned the title of Food Tamed.

Finger Taming: The next step consists of gently trying to stroke the hamster's head using the fingers of one hand while feeding it with the other hand. As soon as the hamster tolerates this without the treat, it is finger tamed.

Hand Taming: When the hamster carefully climbs onto your preferred hand and disappears, sniffing its way up the arm of your jacket, the animal is hand tamed. It is important not to use any force to get your pet to perform this trick. Let the hamster decide for itself how far it wants to go. After a while it will find the warm skin of its caregiver to be pleasant and will seek hand contact on its own.

Note: At first, let the hamster climb from one hand to the other as on stairs. That way it keeps moving, and it can't get back onto the bottom of the cage right away.

Encourage your hamster only near the bottom of the cage, a tabletop, or some other surface as it clambers about on your hand. Hamsters are prone to falling unexpectedly and can be seriously injured by falls from significant heights (see page 73).

Young hamsters like to experiment and need an exercise wheel that won't tip over.

Picking Up, Carrying, Catching

Picking up: If you want to pick up a hamster that is not ready to come to your hand willingly, you should never proceed with force. Above all, don't suddenly grab it from above, or it will feel that it's suddenly been snatched up by a raptor (the seized prey effect). In reaction, it throws itself lightning-quick onto its back and attempts to bite. You must wait until the hamster stops running around and growling and makes no further defensive moves. Then, cup your hands to form a protective cave over the animal and gently lift it up.

Note: Holding the rib cage too tightly can produce a state of shock by compressing the lungs.

Carrying: Always use the cave trick even when carrying the hamster, since it feels a little more secure inside and won't be tempted to jump, as it might if held on an open hand.

Catching: Catching a runaway on the floor can sometimes pose problems. Before the fugitive heads for the heating duct or the space under the refrigerator, scoop it up using your hands and a plastic or cardboard cup. Your hamster will feel secure in the cup and you can easily carry it back to the cage.

Selective Nipping

Hamsters that have been handled gently from infancy will be less likely to bite than will an adult hamster being handled for the first time. If you're not sure about your new pet, wear gardening gloves.

Some hamsters selectively bite some people, but not others. They might feel less

Bits of variously colored corn and grains are components of most prepared feeds.

How much can a hamster learn?

Hamsters are not stupid. You'll realize that quickly. Your hamster will quickly recognize you by your voice and your smell. Hamsters also learn to distinguish among several people. Simone knows that well. Her hamster Nicki immediately disappears into its house when her friend Claudia comes over. Claudia once accidentally stepped on Nicki when he was running around in the room. Ever since that time Nicki wants nothing to do with Claudia. Johnny has a clever hamster. When he placed a small wooden seesaw on the floor, the little fellow quickly figured out how the seesaw worked. The hamster also knows the places in the room where it has gotten treats from Johnny. When the hamster is free to run around in the room, it runs there and waits until Johnny brings it a raisin. Watch how inventive your hamster is when, for example, it wants to bring a big piece of carrot into its house. It may seize the heavy lump at one end with its teeth and drag it backwards as it runs into its house. Or your hamster may have a different, equally clever, strategy.

threatened by a child's small hand than by an adult's large, strong hand.

Entertainment in the Cage

Life in the cage is often monotonous and unnatural for the hamster (see How to Solve Behavior Problems, page 112). That's why it's important to set up the surroundings for the hamster in an appropriate way. You can do this mostly by providing some objects that are related to conditions in the wild.

Give your hamster a cage with several stories, branches for climbing, and ladders. It also needs places to hide in the form of pieces of bark, little boxes, cardboard tubes, and stone slabs, as well as an exercise wheel and a sleeping and storage house (see Useful Accessories, page 49). The inventory of the cage must continually be changed, but a piece at a time—all at once would be too stressful because of all the new smells!

If you can take a familiar toy, along with the piece of bedding, home from the hamster's cage in the pet store, your pet will feel that much more at home in its new cage. Whenever you add a piece of equipment, rub it all over with one the hamster has already used, and your pet will accept each new development.

Appropriate Activities

Give your hamster tasks that correspond to its natural abilities and satisfy its thirst for discovery. Since one of the main purposes of doing this is to get out of familiar territory, you should always combine these activities with the hamster's out-of-cage exercise; leave the cage on the floor so the hamster can get back in when it wishes (see page 58).

Appropriate activities include placing various nesting materials in several locations around the room (see page 87), and setting out food dishes or hand feeding at different places. Offer the hamster leafy twigs and roots stalks for

gnawing, as well as sand and grass clippings in shallow dishes for digging. Set up safe obstacles in the form of barriers for the hamster to climb over. Also a swing, a seesaw, or a maze of tubes or small boxes provides variety. These activities allow you to enjoy your contact with your little friend at the same time.

Interesting Observations

The intriguing thing about hamsters is that they act totally uninhibited after their

TIP

If, in spite of all precautions, a hamster bites down on your finger, try never to fling it off in pain and fear. It could sustain life-threatening injuries. Instead, try to keep cool and put the animal quickly onto the floor of the cage or another surface. Then it will usually let go. Clean and disinfect the puncture wound, and check with your doctor about further treatment.

Hamsters like to use wooden seesaws like this one from the pet store for balancing.

Houses with an incline for climbing stimulate activity.

adjustment phase, and offer a silent observer a comprehensive view of their private life. You should always take the time to watch your hamster, whether it's in the cage or exploring the room during free exercise. You will observe some fascinating things. Its behavior—squirreling away and storing provisions, collecting and carrying nesting material, and building the nest, its intensive grooming, and even its mating behavior offer a wealth of interesting surprises.

The most striking thing is that all this takes place in the smallest space.

While you are enjoying your hamster's antics, however, don't share the experience with your other household pets. If your hamster senses other animals looking through the bars of its cage, it will become fearful and agitated.

111

How to Solve Behavior Problems

Most problems that crop up when humans and hamsters live together are not the fault of the animal, but rather of the people. Such problems are usually rooted in that the way the hamsters are kept is not sufficiently keyed to their natural requirements and habits. As a result, the animals develop abnormal behavior patters. Above all, surroundings that are not set up appropriately can produce displacement activities, which are also described as captivity disorders or cage neuroses.

Stereotypies— Circus Ring Motions

Situation: The hamster runs ceaselessly and frantically back and forth in the front of its cage, climbs in circles as if driven by a motor, or continually jumps up in a corner of the cage. The fixation points, the radius, or the distance of the motions are always the same and are adapted to the size of the cage.
Cause: This kind of behavior is called a stereotypy. The term is used to designate compulsive, usually rhythmical movements that have no purpose or meaning. Because of their similarity to the monotonous motions of trained animals in a circus ring, the term "circus ring motions" was coined. Insufficient room due to restricted cage size, failure to take into account the necessary three-dimensionality of the space, and inadequate exercise cause the animals to compensate in these ways for their natural need for movement.
Remedy: Provide a larger cage and apparatus for daily exercise. Comply with the recommendations for purchasing a cage starting on page 44, and be sure to get a proper exercise wheel (see pages 107 and 115). Although hamsters are essentially nocturnal creatures and will run through the wee hours in a frenzy of stereotypical behavior, they are usually crepuscular, and can be active for periods during the day, as well. If they are encouraged to be more active during daylight hours, they might settle down for at least part of the night.
Note: When a hamster with this kind of disorder is transferred to a larger cage, it will at first retain the familiar motions. But after a while it will adjust to the new surroundings and cease its compulsive behavior.

Biting the Cage

Situation: The hamster gnaws on the bars of the cage, especially at night.
Cause: This behavior also constitutes a certain kind of stereotypy.

Since biting the bars is usually carried on at night, we often find out about it only by noticing the damaged plating on the cage bars. They are gnawed so intensively and repeatedly that the coloring is

Opportunities for activities appropriate to hamsters prevent stereotypies.

112

removed. Cage boredom and lack of stimulation by appropriate cage furnishings are the cause.

Also, too little gnawing material, a lack of lining material for building the nest, and the absence of a water bottle and a salt lick can be causes for gnawing the cage.

<u>Remedy</u>: Set up the cage with lots of variety (see page 109) and check to see that other requirements are met.

Aggressiveness

<u>Situation</u>: The hamster responds defensively to every effort to establish contact and is quick to bite (see Voice and Body Language, page 100).

<u>Cause</u>: Hamsters with this behavioral disorder are often jokingly referred to as "fighting hamsters." The cause of aggressive behavior is, above all, failure to provide the rest time that's vitally important to the hamster. Disturbances include not only checking the nest too

frequently and lifting the hamster out when it's in a deep sleep, but also placing the cage in a location that's brightly lit or too noisy. Other causes can also include a sleeping house that's too small and a lack of nesting material.

<u>Solution</u>: Allow your hamster to sleep undisturbed and provide for its essential needs (see A Place for the Cage, page 44; Sleeping Quarters, page 51; and Nesting Material, page 55).

Note: All these behavioral disorders are remedied most effectively if addressed when they first appear.

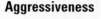

If the problems have turned into substitutes for natural behaviors, many times a belated removal of the cause doesn't produce the desired effect. In essence, that means that a cage biter will remain a cage biter, even if it's provided with gnawing material. Still, you don't want to throw in the towel. Try to accommodate the hamster's needs and be patient. Check again to be sure you are providing all the necessary conditions for keeping hamsters that have been explained so far and improve them as needed (see What Hamsters Need, page 44).

The Hamster Doesn't Become Friendly

Situation: Even though the hamster has lived in the house for several weeks, it still is not friendly. It flees in fear to its house whenever anyone comes near the cage. When it is let out of the cage it scoots under the furniture and spends the entire time hiding.

Causes: Just as with overly aggressive behavior, failure to observe rest periods must also be suspected in cases of excessive fearfulness. The animal doesn't feel safe anywhere and looks everywhere for protection. Also, clumsiness in handling, or an upsetting experience can produce undesirable fearfulness.

Remedy: An anxiety-ridden hamster must slowly learn that no danger threatens from humans. Always approach its cage carefully. Talk softly to the animal. Give it treats by hand. Make sure the cage is set up properly (see information starting on page 44).

Round cages are not recommended for hamsters.

Picking Up the Hamster

Situation: After running around free, the hamster was picked up by the nape of the neck. Suddenly it twisted its head around and bit down hard on the finger of the owner, who, through fear and pain, dropped the hamster. The hamster suffered a broken back and had to be put to sleep.
Cause: By using the thumb and forefinger, it is entirely possible to grab the hamster by the nape of the neck and pick it up. Then it falls into the carrying stiffness (see photos on pages 84–85), just as when it was carried by its mother. You have to grasp the hamster right behind the head; otherwise, it will turn around inside its loose skin and try to bite. So this procedure is rarely advisable to new hamster owners.
Remedy: When you want to pick up the hamster, use both hands to form a kind of cave over the animal and wait until

The Roborowski dwarf hamster is not much bigger than a leaf of parsley.

it calms down. Then close your hands and pick up the hamster. The cave gives it a sense of security.

The Exercise Wheel

Situation: When the hamster is running in its wheel, the squeaking can become very annoying, especially because this occurs at night. Things can get so bad that the whole cage is banished to an out-of-the-way room because the children can't get to sleep. The hamster may also get a paw caught so badly that it limps for several days.
Cause: The exercise wheel doesn't make the grade. A properly built wheel moves without making a racket and is constructed in such a way as to pose no danger of injury.
Remedy: From among the many available exercise wheels, choose one made of

nickel-plated or galvanized metal. Dipped wheels are not recommended because the colored coating doesn't stand up to hamster teeth. Exercise wheels made of plastic certainly are inexpensive, but they often get chewed up and soon don't work properly. Also any pieces of plastic that get swallowed, such as spokes of the wheel, remain in the hamster's rumen and can cause chronic digestive disorders. In order to prevent injuries, the wheel must allow free access on one side and be closed on the pivot side (see drawing on page 49 and photo on page 53). You should also pay attention to the size of the exercise wheel. The dimensions of a wheel are often too small for golden hamsters. This forces the animal to run in an unnatural posture with a bowed back. In the long

115

run, this can damage the spine. Check to see that the exercise wheel has a solid stand. Test it to be sure that it turns quietly and without wobbling. The mesh of some exercise wheels often makes the whole cage vibrate and produces unpleasant buzzing noises.

Note: Running in the exercise wheel constitutes a kind of stereotypy. Along with ceaseless running back and forth along one side of the cage and gnawing the bars for hours on end, it is another behavior disorder connected to living in the cage. That's why providing an exercise wheel is a double-edged sword. On one hand, it affords the chance to get sufficient exercise, but on the other, it may cause a behavior disorder that can turn into a real obsession. Animals like that get so dependent on running for a long time that they experience withdrawal symptoms when the wheel is suddenly taken away. The hamster misses the exercise wheel even if you replace it with a larger cage or additional climbing apparatus. So consider carefully whether you really want to get an exercise wheel for your hamster. Of course, the ideal situation is

for the hamster to be able to run around free in a safe room of the home in the evening or at night (see page 58). Then it won't need an exercise wheel. But free-running hamsters often squeeze through cracks or grates and end up inside the walls. If your pet has to spend most of its time in the cage, you can't avoid getting an exercise wheel.

Dangerous Toys

<u>Situation:</u> Under the name "Hamster Ball" and "Hamster Car," toys are available that supposedly will banish boredom in children and hamsters (see photo, page 117). These toys are constructed so that the hamster is closed in and provides locomotion by running.

The more the hamster tries to get out of the tiny space, the faster it goes and the more it needs the air that comes in only through small openings in the sides. Imagine the possibilities if the whole ball or car, with the hamster inside, falls off the table because children help it along by giving it a push. Every

veterinarian has sad tales to tell about life-threatening injuries that have happened this way. Even if the hamster is not physically injured, the apparatus is more torture chamber than toy for the frightened animal.

<u>Remedy:</u> Play is supposed to be activity for amusement and for passing time. Children must learn that what is fun for them is not necessarily fun for an animal. Hamsters don't get excited about playthings that by appearance and nature are designed for children to enjoy. Hamsters prefer "toys" such as tubes of dried grass with openings for crawling in and out (see photo on page 113) or playthings of wood such as a polygon with several holes drilled in it (see page 72) or a seesaw (see page 110).

With hamsters, everything that looks like play arises from their exploratory behavior. Once they have completely explored a climbing apparatus, they lose interest in it. Hamsters like variety in their environment. Even in the wild, a hamster's habitat changes all the time. All that's required for that is a couple of strong gusts of wind or a sudden downpour.

That's why, in order to prevent cage boredom, you should regularly provide new objects for sniffing, crawling through, hiding in, climbing, and investigating (see pages 109–110), but never change too much at one time.

In choosing such objects always be wary of possible dangers or toxic substances in the form of glues or paints.

Note: Explain to children that imprisoning the hamster in a dollhouse or forcing it to ride an electric train causes the same stress as the "Hamster Ball" or the "Hamster Car."

Aging

Situation: The hamster spends more and more time in the evenings in its sleeping house, no longer frequents its exercise wheel, squirrels away very little food, moves unsteadily, loses weight, and has an unkempt, unattractive coat.

Cause: The hamster's aging process has begun. One day you'll find it lifeless in its nest or in a corner of the cage.

Solution: Especially for children, the loss of a beloved hamster can be painful. If you have followed the advice in this book, you will have explained to your children when you first purchased the pet that the

nimble, intense hamster needs just two years to fulfill all its duties, whereas most humans need 70 or 80 years. Still, even if you have properly prepared the family for the pet's short life span, experiencing its death will make the children as well as the adults sad for a while. My suggestion is this: Explain that being sad about a loved one's death is a natural part of life. Take turns sharing happy memories of the pet—everyone gets a turn, even the youngest child. Then plan together the things you will do to make the life of your next pet, perhaps another hamster, even better.

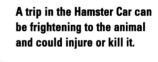

A trip in the Hamster Car can be frightening to the animal and could injure or kill it.

My Hamster

This space is for your favorite picture.

_____

Name

Date of Birth

Breeder/Pet Store

Sex

Breed/Color

Weight

Markings

Favorite Foods

Favorite Activity

Name, Address, and Phone Number of Veterinarian

Sometimes hamsters overestimate their climbing ability and sustain serious injuries.

121

A brick can be used to create a second story inside the hamster cage.

**Teeth and
forepaws
are used to
transport
large chunks.**

How to Learn More

If you have specific questions about your hamster's health or behavior, you should first consult your local veterinarian. The pet shop where you bought your hamster should also be able to help. Your town or school library may have other helpful books, and the interlibrary loan service usually can produce needed resources that your local library doesn't own. Some state and county agricultural fairs have exhibits devoted to small rodents, and they may offer opportunities to get acquainted with and learn from other people who share your interest. Further ideas for networking and special projects may include 4-H, scouting, and other clubs and organizations.

Helpful Books

Barrie, Anmarie. *Hamsters: For Those Who Care.* Neptune, NJ: TFH Publications, 1994.

Evans, Mark and Roger A. Caras. *Hamster (ASPCA Pet Care Guides for Kids).* London: DK Publishing, 1993.

Mays, Marianne. *Proper Care of Hamsters.* Neptune, NJ: TFH Publications, 1994.

Petty, Kate. *Hamsters: First Pet Series.* Hauppauge, NY: Barron's Educational Series, 1993.

Siino, Betsy S. *The Hamster: An Owner's Guide to a Happy, Healthy Pet.* New York, NY: Howell Book House, 1997.

von Frisch, Otto. *Hamsters: A Complete Pet Owner's Manual.* Hauppauge, NY: Barron's Educational Series, 1989.

Web Sites and Newsgroups

The Animal Council
www.fanciers.com/npa

National Animal Interest Alliance
ww.naiaonline.org

Responsible Pet Owners Alliance
NOAH@express-news.net

The Author

Peter Hollmann, DMV, studied veterinary medicine in Munich, Germany. He is an expert in animal reproduction. Since 1971 he has run a veterinary clinic in Bad Tolz-Wolfratshausen, where he specializes in small pets. Ever since his childhood, his greatest fondness has been for small rodents, and he is devoted to their care and welfare. He is known to a wide audience through numerous publications, educational programs, and radio and television broadcasts.

The Photographer

The photos in this book are by Karin Skogstad, with the following exceptions:
Hollmann: Pages 78, 79, 114, 117; Reinhard: Pages 36 top; 37 top left and top right; 38 top left and top right; 39 top left; 40 top left and top right; 41 top; 80; Wegler: Page 95
Karin Skogstad has been working since 1979 as a freelance journalist and photographer. Her specialties are animals and plants.

The Artist

Renate Holzner works as a freelance illustrator in Regensburg, Germany. Her extensive repertory includes line drawings, photographically realistic illustrations, and computer graphics.

The Translator

Eric A. Bye, M.A., is a freelance translator who lives and works in Vermont. He translates primarily from German, French, and Spanish into English.

Cover Photos

Pages 2 and 3: A clay pot like this one makes a great hiding place for hamsters.
Pages 6 and 7: Everything that's hollow and enclosed is explored with curiosity.
Pages 42–43: Be careful that the hamster doesn't fall. That's how many hamsters kept as house pets have died.
Pages 92–93: This albino hamster grooms itself thoroughly after its extended sleep.
Back cover: A juicy cucumber slice quenches thirst.

Acknowlegment

The publisher would like to thank Dan F. Rice, D.V.M., for sharing his small-animal expertise in the preparation of this book.

English translation copyright ©1999 by Barron's Educational Series, Inc. Original title of the book in German is *Der Hamster* Copyright ©1998 Grafe und Unzer Verlag GmbH, Munich

Translation from the German by Eric A. Bye

All inquiries should be addressed to:
Barron's Educational Series, Inc.
250 Wireless Boulevard
Hauppauge, NY 11788
http://www.barronseduc.com

Library of Congress Catalog Card No. 98-46014

International Standard Book No. 0-7641-5160-6

Library of Congress Cataloging-in-Publication Data

Hollmann, Peter.
  [Hamsters. English]
  Hamsters : how to care for them, feed them, and understand them / Peter Hollmann ; photographs by Karin Stogstad ; illustrated by Renate Holzner ; translated from the German by Eric A Bye.
    p.   cm. — (Family pet)
  ISBN 0-7641-5160-6
  1. Hamsters as pets. I. Title. II. Series.
SF459.H3H6513   1999
636.935'6—dc21   98-46014
                            CIP

Printed in Hong Kong
9 8 7 6 5 4 3 2 1

Important Note

Any time your hamster shows symptoms of illness (see pages 74 and 75) you should take it to the veterinarian without delay. Some illnesses are communicable to humans and can be serious (see pages 78–79). If in doubt, or if your hamster has bitten you, consult a doctor.

Some people are allergic to animal hair. If you're not sure, ask your doctor before getting a hamster.

Pet shops sell dried fruits for small rodents.

127